HOW TO LOVE YOURSELF

FOR HAPPINESS AND SUCCESS

AN AUTHENTIC GUIDE AND WORKBOOK TO INCREASE SELF-CONFIDENCE, FORGIVE THE PAST, STOP TOXIC EMOTIONS, AND OVERCOME NEGATIVITY TO LIVE WITH MORE PEACE

DYLAN WALKER

© Copyright 2023 - All rights reserved.

The content contained within this book may not be reproduced, duplicated, or transmitted without direct written permission from the author or the publisher.

Under no circumstances will any blame or legal responsibility be held against the publisher or author for any damages, reparation, or monetary loss due to the information contained within this book, either directly or indirectly.

Legal Notice

This book is copyright protected. It is only for personal use. You may not amend, distribute, sell, use, quote, or paraphrase any part, or the content within this book, without the consent of the author or publisher.

Disclaimer Notice

Please note the information contained within this document is for educational and entertainment purposes only. All effort has been executed to present accurate, up-to-date, reliable, and complete information. No warranties of any kind are declared or implied. Readers acknowledge that the author is not engaged in the rendering of legal, financial, medical, or professional advice. The content within this book has been derived from various sources. Please consult a licensed professional before attempting any techniques outlined in this book.

By reading this document, the reader agrees that under no circumstances is the author responsible for any losses, direct or indirect, that are incurred as a result of the use of the information contained within this document, including, but not limited to, errors, omissions, or inaccuracies.

YOUR FREE GIFT

As a way of saying thanks for your purchase, I'm offering the book Overcoming Limiting Beliefs for FREE to my readers.
To get instant access just go to:

https://dylanwalkerbooks.com/selflove-free-bonus

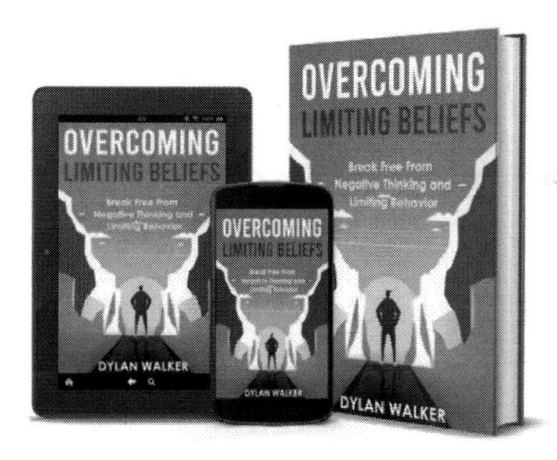

Inside the book, you will discover:

- ➤ **10 steps to break through your limiting beliefs**: Even if you struggled with negative thinking before, this book will be the change you need.

- ➤ **An action plan to end sabotaging yourself**: Learn exactly how to reframe your thoughts with just 10-minutes a day.

- ➤ **Reduce stress and achieve unshakable confidence**: A healthy mindset leads to achieving your goals and dreams. It's time to take back your life!

If you want to stop negative thinking and start making progress towards your dreams make sure to grab the free book.

TABLE OF CONTENTS

INTRODUCTION 1

CHAPTER 1: The "Taboo" of Self-Love 4
    What Self-Love Is 5
    What Self-Love Is Not 7
    Why Society Cringes at Self-Love 8
    The Relationship Between Self-Love, Happiness, and Success 10
    Lizzo's Story—Finding Self-Love 13
    Key Takeaways 14
    Practical Activity—Create a Self-Care Kit 15

CHAPTER 2: You Matter and Your Dreams Are Valid 17
    What Does Success Really Mean? 17
    Creative Success—James McAvoy's Story 23
    Are My Dreams Worth Anything? 25
    Factors That Can Undermine Your Dreams 27
    Success Against the Odds—Eminem's Story 30
    Key Takeaways 31
    Practical Activity—Create Your Own Definition of Success 33

CHAPTER 3: Overcoming Negativity The First Steps 35
    How Negativity Starts and Grows 35
    Discovering the Root Causes of Your Negativity 41
    Inner Critic Reworking (How to Turn the Voice in Your Head into a Friend) 43

	Emma Stone's Story—Dealing With Her Inner Critic	46
	Key Takeaways	47
	Worksheet: Overcoming Negative Thinking	48
	Worksheet: Dealing with Your Inner Critic	51
CHAPTER 4:	Low Self-Esteem Leads to Self-Neglect	54
	What Is Self-Neglect?	55
	How Low Self-Esteem Breeds Unhappiness	57
	What Is Imposter Syndrome?	58
	How Low Self-Esteem Encourages Failure	59
	Being a Pushover Is Not Attractive	61
	How to Say "No" to Self-Neglect and Codependency	64
	Key Takeaways	67
	Worksheet: Overcoming Low Self-Esteem	68
CHAPTER 5:	Forgive the Past, Forgive Yourself	70
	The Benefits of Forgiveness	71
	The Importance of Forgiving the Past	72
	Oprah Winfrey's Story—Self-forgiveness	78
	Key Takeaways	79
	Worksheet: Forgiveness and Self-Forgiveness	80
CHAPTER 6:	Decluttering for a Happy and Stress-Free Life	82
	What Is Mind Decluttering?	83
	How Decluttering Impacts Happiness and Success	84
	How to Do a Thorough Mind Declutter	87
	How to Do a Thorough Relationship Declutter	89
	Key Takeaways	92
	Activity—Declutter Your Relationships	93
CHAPTER 7:	Stop Toxic Emotions and Build Positivity	94
	Why Emotions Are Useful	94
	Meaning and Examples of Toxic Emotions	99
	How Toxic Emotions Impact Happiness	101
	Why You Must Deal With Toxic Emotions	103
	Key Takeaways	104
	Activity: Get in Touch with Your Emotions	105

CHAPTER 8: Self-Care, Peace of Mind, and Daily Happiness.............. 107

All-Around Guide to Self-Care And Happiness 108

Managing Disappointment and Sad Situations................................117

How to Ensure Your Peace of Mind Every Day 119

Daily Exercises for Happiness... 121

Key Takeaways 125

Activity: Create a Self-Care Plan... 127

CONCLUSION..129
ABOUT THE AUTHOR 131
REFERENCES... 133

INTRODUCTION

Talented actress and singer Selena Gomez has admitted to struggling with self-love throughout her career. She has talked about how her battle with the autoimmune disease lupus has taken a toll on her mental health and has made it increasingly difficult for her to feel confident and secure in herself. Besides this, she is constantly scrutinized by the media and her fans, which has served to increase her feelings of insecurity and self-doubt, especially after recent comments about her weight gain. The weight gain is a result of the medication she has to use to stay healthy.

Selena has advocated for mental health awareness and has talked about the importance of self-care. She has put a lot of effort into sharing her self-love journey with her followers. Selena has become an inspiration for many who struggle with low self-esteem and has shown that even celebrities struggle with accepting themselves and that they're also affected by ill health and other challenges.

Self-love is such an essential aspect of our lives; nevertheless, many of us struggle to love and value ourselves, for various reasons. Whether we have health struggles like Selena, or we simply care too much about what others think about us, it can truly be a struggle to accept and appreciate ourselves.

This battle with ourselves often has its origin in childhood and the communication we received from our childhood caregivers. If you had overbearing and critical adults in your life, you could struggle with your self-esteem and may have developed negative self-talk and a critical inner voice.

The demands of daily life and societal pressures can also make it challenging to love ourselves fully. How many times have you wanted to take some time out for yourself, just to do something simple, but you always feel like you have other commitments and responsibilities? When it comes to looking after ourselves, it may often feel like we're last on the long to-do list. If you're a parent with many kids who depend on you, it can be especially challenging to find time for self-care.

In this book, we explore practical strategies and tools that will help you cultivate self-esteem, and overcome any obstacles and challenges that could be holding you back. We'll help you see that you deserve to make time for yourself to look after your own needs and desires. After all, you can't look after others if you're burned out and feel like you have nothing more to give.

There are many practical things you can do to make progress on your exciting self-love adventure. We discuss practices and exercises that can help you develop an appreciation for yourself such as affirmations, self-care, and practicing mindfulness.

Whether you're just starting on your journey, or you want to cultivate more self-love, this book offers you inspiration and advice to help you love and appreciate yourself more fully. You will realize that it isn't selfish to give yourself the attention you need. Placing yourself at the top of your list will also ultimately help you to build better relationships with others.

INTRODUCTION

This book will act as a roadmap on your path to self-discovery and will empower you to break free from the constraints of your past and embrace a brighter future. It doesn't matter if your past was full of negative experiences and failures; you have the power to reach out to a positive future and claim it for yourself.

If you feel you are ready to embark on a journey of self-realization and unleash your full potential, then this book is for you. Transform your life—and experience the joy, love, and success that you deserve!

CHAPTER 1:
THE "TABOO" OF SELF-LOVE

Self-love is more important than ever before in our modern world. We're facing unprecedented levels of anxiety, stress, and uncertainty; self-confidence can help us improve our resilience to cope with all these challenges.

Even though it has many benefits, self-love is often misunderstood by people, and even stigmatized by society. Some see loving ourselves as selfish, and even narcissistic. Those of us who prioritize our well-being could discover that we're being judged and criticized by others. This could cause shame and guilt, which could make it difficult to practice loving ourselves.

Social media, and the media in general, have also perpetuated unrealistic beauty ideals that constantly encourage us to compare ourselves to others and make it difficult to love ourselves as we are.

To change attitudes and perceptions, we need to realize that self-love is an essential aspect of our well-being. When we pay attention to our needs and practice self-care, we're better able to show up as our best selves for others and make a positive impact in the world.

If your self-esteem is strong, you'll also experience more empathy for others. People who are burned-out struggle to feel compassion for those around them; if you're well-rested and have practiced self-care, you'll be more able to feel love and compassion for other people.

The path to loving yourself isn't always an easy journey, and you may experience many bumps on the road.

It's a lifelong commitment, as you need to be able to show yourself kindness on most days. It will be easier to take the time to care for yourself on some days than others, especially during busy and stressful periods. Don't be too hard on yourself if you can't take care of yourself in a healthy way, every day. You definitely shouldn't be adding more stress to your life.

What Self-Love Is

Loving ourselves involves an appreciation and acceptance of ourselves including both our positive qualities and imperfections. If we truly love ourselves, we'll treat ourselves with respect, kindness, and compassion. We'll be able to recognize our needs and deal with them. This includes our physical, emotional, and spiritual needs. We must make time to engage in activities that promote personal growth and well-being.

Self-love is about having a positive relationship with yourself. You need to value yourself enough that you will practice self-care activities such as sleeping and exercising enough, eating healthy food, and spending time doing things that you enjoy.

It also has to do with having boundaries and the ability to say "no" to people and activities that won't benefit your well-being. Sufficient self-reflection can help you build greater self-awareness and confidence, which will allow you to ultimately lead a more fulfilling life.

When your self-esteem is high, you'll also be able to have more gratifying relationships with others, and you won't be afraid to let those close to you experience your authentic personality. You won't feel the need to present a false facade to the world, while constantly trying to please others according to the expectations they have of you. You will also attract more positive and supportive people into your life.

The Hard Road to Self-Love

Self-appreciation can also make you more resilient in the long run, which will help you when it comes to dealing with challenges and moving on from difficult situations.

You can only truly appreciate and love yourself if you know yourself better. It's important to spend time alone and tune into your hopes, dreams, and goals. If you're hurting, you need to know why you're in pain.

While it's important to have confidence and good self-esteem, you don't have to feel good about yourself all the time. There's no need to judge yourself when you have days when you feel as if you don't like yourself, or you think you should have achieved more by the age you are. You're only human, and we all go through these feelings and the occasional attack of depressing, negative thoughts. The problem comes in when you experience this on a daily basis.

Remember that loving yourself doesn't necessarily mean you have to lead a problem-free and stress-free life. It's about doing difficult things to create the best kind of life possible for yourself. It can also be about doing things that aren't that enjoyable, but are the best for you, at a certain stage of your life.

This involves creating an authentic life and letting go of some past experiences that could still have a hold on you.

Building self-esteem and gaining self-confidence is also a part of growing up. It's about taking personal responsibility and making sure you get what you need, to be able to function as a productive human being who can manage healthy relationships with others.

What Self-Love Is Not

Some people might tell you that you're selfish or self-absorbed if you take time for yourself and practice self-care. However, this is a total misconception, and you shouldn't listen to them.

This idea—which stubbornly persists in some parts of the world today—that it's wrong, and possibly even immoral, to put your needs above those of others comes from cultural and societal beliefs that prioritize putting others first.

Some people also see self-love as a form of narcissism, where you just tend to focus on yourself at all times, at the expense of the needs of others. However, an important difference is that narcissists tend to abuse others, which you won't do if you truly love yourself. It may just be that you have been unlucky, and have met people who have had negative experiences with others, where those others were too focused on their own needs to be concerned about anyone else's. For example, individuals who were constantly ignored by their parents as children, and who preferred to pursue their own pleasures, may equate self-love to selfishness.

If you're a woman, you might, unfortunately, find that societal expectations and pressure are even worse when it comes to loving yourself. Women are still, in many instances, expected to prioritize the needs of everyone else above their own, as they are still often seen as the caretakers of everyone around them. Women who refuse to stay in this mold may be labeled "selfish."

However, women should challenge these stereotypes, as they also have the right to see to their own needs, and do things that promote their personal growth.

There are a whole bunch of other things that self-love is *not*.

It's *not* about indulging in unhealthy behaviors and habits. Instead, it's about treating yourself with kindness and respect, which will allow you to make the right choices for your emotional, mental, and physical well-being.

Self-love is also *not* about being perfect. It's about accepting yourself with your flaws and imperfections. It also shouldn't be used as another excuse to get down on yourself, if you can't instantly create the perfect life with abundant self-esteem. The idea is not to put more pressure on you, or to give you something else to live up to. It's simply to remind you that you're fine the way you are and that you're a perfectly acceptable and lovable human being, even if you may have a bad temper from time to time! So, please don't make a list with all the requirements you need to meet for loving yourself. Just look after yourself, be kind to yourself, and let things happen naturally. If you don't like yourself every single minute of the day, that's okay, too.

Why Society Cringes at Self-Love

Even though it's vital for mental and emotional well-being, society still cringes at the idea of self-love. There is still a stigma attached to the idea, as people may feel they will be regarded as selfish if they acknowledge their needs and desires.

THE "TABOO" OF SELF-LOVE

It can be difficult to feel good about yourself in a society that emphasizes success and external validation. People can feel inadequate and doubt themselves as a result of the pressure to achieve certain beauty standards, such as a slender and toned body, as well as wealth and success.

If you consider self-admiration in this context, it can be seen as a reflection of societal norms and expectations. It, therefore, becomes extremely difficult for some people to embrace this concept since they want to feel a part of society or even a certain group.

When women take time to care for themselves, it is—in some cases—still viewed as an act of resistance against societal norms. While it's considered desirable to encourage children to love themselves, it's not that simple once you become an adult.

These social norms are often rooted in ideas about gender and race, but the other unfortunate truth is that self-love is bad for business. Many lucrative industries in our modern society have been built on people's lack of self-visualization and struggle with self-confidence, especially that of women.

The makeup and clothing industry is known for promoting unrealistic beauty standards and, sometimes, unattainable ideals that can lead to low self-esteem and confidence. However, while some are promoting body positivity and diversity, in many cases they now promote an ideal bigger body type—for example, a plus-size woman with wide hips and big buttocks, but with a flat stomach. The weight loss industry has also benefited, for many years, from promoting an ideal body image when it came to selling special diets and "medicine" to people—that, in some cases, have turned out to be harmful and, in many cases, don't work. Gymnasiums have benefited from selling desperate customers expensive contracts that can't be canceled and, often, end up being used not more than a few times.

However, in the end, people are responsible for their own self-care and well-being. While some businesses may contribute to negative emotions, it's up to each person to take control of their emotional health.

The pressure to conform to societal expectations and norms is a big challenge in our world today. It could cause you to start feeling inadequate, which in turn can unfavorably impact your mental health. High self-esteem can help you navigate the world with more confidence.

Self-assurance can also make you more accepting and grateful for the life you already have. If you're capable of taking more responsibility for our life and actions, you'll be able to lead a more fulfilling and authentic life. You'll also become more satisfied with your life if you realize that you can determine how you live it. Being content with your life will contribute to overall lower levels of stress.

The Relationship Between Self-Love, Happiness, and Success

Self-love, happiness, and success are all related and can influence one another.

Loving and accepting yourself can be regarded as the foundation of happiness. If you take pride and revel in yourself, you'll feel happier and more confident. You'll be able to lead a happier life in the long term, and your positive self-image will help you develop a more enthusiastic outlook on life. You'll also become more resilient when it comes to dealing with, and recovering from, setbacks and challenges.

It will become easier for you to achieve success in your life. You'll have a clearer idea of your strengths and weaknesses, and you'll know what goals

THE "TABOO" OF SELF-LOVE

you can realistically achieve. Self-love can also help you when it comes to overcoming self-sabotage and fear.

You're more likely to achieve success if you lead a happy and satisfying life, as you'll be more productive and motivated. Happiness can also improve your physical health since you'll be more motivated to exercise and eat healthily.

Why Self-Love Is Necessary for Happiness

It can be difficult to find the time to truly value yourself, especially since we lead such busy lives today. It always seems like there is something more important to do, and there are so many other people to take care of before you can get to yourself.

The effects of a lack of self-love can be extremely detrimental to your well-being. People who struggle with this are usually less resilient, struggling with high stress levels and anxiety, and becoming upset by every little thing that goes wrong in their lives. Everything can feel more difficult and overwhelming, and they end up feeling depleted.

Self-importance can be difficult to learn, and it takes practice—especially if you're a people pleaser by nature, who keeps putting everyone else's needs before your own. The sad fact is that, if you keep on putting everyone else before yourself, you're going to end up in a place where you feel resentful of others, unhappy, and as if you're unsuccessful in life.

One of the things that often get in the way of our self-confidence is comparing ourselves with others. This is a pointless exercise since we all have different personalities and abilities. By doing this, you're setting yourself up for disappointment, and even heartache. Before you compare yourself with friends or family members on social media, keep in mind that people usually only post their successes on social media. People like to brag about accomplishments, such as being able to afford a fancy lifestyle, but they don't often want to tell others about failures, such as losing their jobs.

We often feel inferior when we compare ourselves to others who have more than we have. However, you'll be much happier in life if you're grateful for what you have.

You'll also be gratified if the life you're living is aligned with your personal values. If you don't have sufficient self-love, it might mean that you're not giving sufficient attention to all these values in your life.

For example, if you struggle to fulfill your obligation to yourself, you might struggle to live in line with your other values, such as your family values. If you're feeling depleted because you never take time to care for yourself, you'll become irritated with your family or too tired to spend time with them.

People who love themselves are usually confident and not scared to state their opinions. They're also able to forgive themselves for their flaws and don't criticize themselves harshly for making mistakes.

It's entirely possible to lose your confidence, and if you're too critical of yourself, you're probably going to be the same with others. You can regain your pride by treating yourself with more compassion.

In summary, happiness, self-love, and success all go together. You're more likely to be successful in life if you're happy and you practice self-love. The elements reinforce each other, and you're also more likely to be happy if you're successful.

THE "TABOO" OF SELF-LOVE

Lizzo's Story—Finding Self-Love

Lizzo—the plus-sized American singer, rapper, and flutist—has been open about her journey towards self-love, and the mental struggles she had to overcome with being frequently attacked by the media about her weight.

Lizzo has managed to find self-love in some of the following ways:

- Lizzo practices self-care by doing things she enjoys such as taking baths, listening to music, and spending time with friends and family. She also makes sure to prioritize her mental and physical health by exercising and eating healthily.
- Lizzo is proud of her body and embraces it fully, even though she has received a lot of criticism in the media and is frequently targeted on social platforms. She often shares photos and videos of herself on social media, showing off her curves and encouraging her fans to love their bodies.
- She surrounds herself with people who uplift and support her. She has said that her team and close friends are her biggest supporters, and she feels grateful to have them in her life.
- The star challenges beauty standards by being unapologetically herself. She has said that she wants to create a space where people can feel accepted and loved, regardless of their size or appearance.
- Lizzo's music often centers on themes of self-love and empowerment. She has written songs such as "Good as Hell" and "Juice," which encourage listeners to love themselves and celebrate their unique qualities.

This Grammy Award winner believes in empowering others as much as possible; she launched the shapewear brand *Yitty* in 2022 and recently launched gender-affirming shapewear for gender-diverse people.

Key Takeaways

> - Self-love is important in the modern world, as we face high levels of anxiety and stress. It can help us become more resilient to cope with these issues.
> - Appreciating ourselves is often misunderstood by society, and mistakenly seen as selfish.
> - We may sometimes be judged and criticized by others for prioritizing our well-being.
> - The media in general, have been perpetuating unrealistic beauty standards that cause people to compare themselves with others and make it even more difficult to love themselves.
> - Another reason why self-love is important in our hectic modern lives is that it helps us see others more compassionately and treat them with empathy.
> - The most basic definition of self-love is that it's an appreciation and acceptance of ourselves, our positive qualities, and our imperfections. It's about having a positive relationship with ourselves.
> - Self-love can help us set boundaries and have more fulfilling relationships with others.
> - We can only truly experience self-love when we spend time on our own to do introspection.

- It's important to remember that it's not about feeling good all the time. We shouldn't judge ourselves if we feel down on some days.
- There is still a belief that it's wrong to put our own needs above those of others.
- Women who refuse to fit into the mold of being caregivers to everyone else may still be labeled as selfish.
- Self-love, happiness, and success are related and can influence one another.
- A positive outlook can help us achieve success in life.
- Never compare yourself to others, as this can be detrimental to your self-love, and can make you lose your confidence in your abilities.

Practical Activity—Create a Self-Care Kit

You can practice your self-love by creating a self-care kit. Start by selecting any type of container that you find attractive. This could be anything from a small box to a decorated basket.

Place items that bring you joy and comfort in your self-care kit container. Some examples are:

- Your favorite books or copies of magazines
- Snacks or treats, preferably as healthy as possible
- A journal and a pen for writing down your thoughts and feelings. Choose a beautifully decorated book that will motivate you to write in it.

- A water bottle or energy drink to keep you hydrated and energized
- A playlist of your favorite songs or music you can use for meditation
- Skincare products you enjoy using, such as a face mask
- Vitamins for when you need an extra boost
- Scented candles are really helpful
- Eye mask for relaxation

Keep your kit where it's easily accessible when you need it—for example, in your desk drawer or nightstand.

Schedule some time in your day when you can use these items. It doesn't have to be a long period; you can take a few minutes to refresh yourself, during times when you're very busy and stressed.

Never feel guilty for taking some time to enjoy things that make you feel good and love yourself more. You're showing yourself love and compassion by taking care of your physical and emotional well-being.

CHAPTER 2:
YOU MATTER AND YOUR DREAMS ARE VALID

Your dreams are important, even if you think you're too old to achieve them or that all your attention should be focused on your family once you become a parent.

Aspirations are crucial, and you need to nurture them and take steps to turn them into a reality. Only *you* can ultimately achieve *your* dreams and goals.

Having dreams also helps us to set goals and work towards achieving them. Dreams can help us stay motivated, even when faced with challenges and obstacles. If you have a specific target, even if it seems unachievable, it can help you visualize the future you want and create a roadmap to get there.

What Does Success Really Mean?

Success can mean different things to different people. If you want to know what it means, you first have to define what it means to you. Don't be too worried if you find this difficult to do. It's never too late to write a new definition for success or to start over if you find your true passion in life later on.

Achievement doesn't necessarily have to involve money, titles, or fame. It should be about what motivates you, makes you happy, and helps you find a sense of purpose. Sometimes, we try too hard to do things to please others, and then we end up being unsuccessful. You might even find that you achieve true success through something you really enjoy, even if it took you a little bit longer to get started. Success might come a bit later to you, if you've lost several years in jobs worrying if you'd be doing the right thing if you resign and do something you'd find more meaningful, such as starting your own business.

Does Success Have a Timeline?

You're never too old to succeed and it's entirely possible to achieve success at any age. Age shouldn't stop you from pursuing your goals and dreams.

There are multiple benefits to pursuing success later in life. Once you're a bit older, you have more life experience, skills, and knowledge—which could be useful in many fields and greatly increase your chances of success. You may also have a better idea of what you want to achieve and how to do it. This can help you stay focused on achieving your goals.

Success is ultimately not determined by age, but more by factors such as a willingness to work hard, dedication, and a lifelong learning mentality. It's never too late to achieve success; for example, the creator of Marvel comics, Stan Lee, only started reaching fruition in his 40s with his comic books. Alan Rickman, the infamous Professor Snape from the hugely successful Harry Potter movies, only made his acting debut at the age of 41.

Other successful people were older than 50 when they started pursuing their dreams. In a sense, you must anticipate when you're ready for victory, work hard, and it will come to you.

When it comes to achieving success, you must stop comparing yourself to other people. Everyone has their own definitions of the term.

Different Definitions of Success

You could measure your success by the activities that motivate and energize you throughout your day. The types of activities that keep us going are usually the ones for which we have a natural talent.

You'll often find that triumph won't come to you if you keep on trying to excel at certain things for the wrong reasons. Maybe you keep making excuses that you have to keep doing things that you don't enjoy that much because you're scared of what will happen when you're successful at something you enjoy and for which you have a talent.

Remember that, even if you achieve great feats, it's important to stay humble and keep working hard. Part of being self-confident is not letting success give you an overinflated ego.

Some people have been raised to believe that success is out of reach and that they shouldn't strive to be anything or aim high because they're simply not good enough, and their dreams are unrealistic. Unfortunately, this mindset can lead to low self-esteem and negative self-talk that can set you back for a long time.

Maybe you've been raised to only chase jobs that will offer you the most money, even though you don't find them fulfilling. For example, maybe you have always wanted to be a successful writer or artist, but because of your family background, your self-talk is negative and you believe this is an impossible dream that won't come true. Your lack of confidence possibly also convinces you that you don't deserve to be successful as a writer.

Instead, you keep going after jobs for which you have some skill, but which don't motivate you as much as writing. You find editor jobs that pay you well but, after a while, you get burned out and you will find it difficult to continue.

If you find yourself in a position like this, you need to sit down and redefine what success means to you. You could potentially earn well as an editor for a while until you start suffering from burnout. Is earning well in a job with an impressive title your definition of success, even if your heart is not in it?

It could take you a while to build up a thriving business as a writer and to start earning, but it's well worth looking into if this is your passion in life and fits in with your definition of success.

Your Journey to Success

What could help you on your journey to success is to first make up your mind about the type of success you want to achieve.

Before you can achieve the goal that is meaningful to you, you need to understand and value yourself, by also taking note of your current strengths and skills. You also need to understand why you want to achieve success. Do you want money and fame, or do you want these things because you think they'll make you happy?

If you can describe what fits in with your definition of success, you'll be able to achieve it on your own terms.

Examples of Different Types of Success

Success isn't just about power, fame, or money. Here are a few examples of different types of success:

- ➢ **Career success** refers to achieving professional goals and accomplishments, such as a promotion or being appointed to a management position.
- ➢ **Academic success** means high grades, completing a degree, or getting an award or scholarship.
- ➢ **Financial success** would mainly refer to achieving financial stability and independence, through investing money or running successful business ventures.
- ➢ Everything doesn't have to be about money and career; **personal success** is often more meaningful to many people. This type of success is about achieving personal goals—such as learning new skills—or quitting bad habits—such as smoking.
- ➢ **Creative success** could potentially also be part of career success. This type of success is focused on artistic and creative achievements, such as producing a great work of art, writing a bestseller, or making a groundbreaking film.
- ➢ Some people might find that **spiritual success** becomes increasingly important to them as they get older, or as they go through life-changing experiences—such as losing a loved one or being diagnosed with a serious illness—that makes them question the meaning of life. This type of success could be about achieving inner peace, mindfulness, gaining spiritual growth through religious rituals, and practices such as meditation and yoga.

Can You Be Happy and Successful at the Same Time?

It's entirely possible to be happy and successful at the same time but is sometimes difficult to achieve.

As said before, you need to define success on your own terms, and it has to align with your values and aspirations. There is no use in comparing yourself to others and feeling that you have to measure up to what they have achieved.

Be as positive as you can. Positive emotions will boost your general well-being, which makes it more likely that you'll achieve success in the long term. While working hard to attain your goals, make time to do things you enjoy, as this will also help you to feel more grateful for the good things you already have in your life.

The goals that you set for yourself need to be realistic. Achievable goals can help you find purpose and direction. You can also break your goals down into smaller steps and milestones to make them more realistic.

Make sure you have a support network and develop strong relationships with family, friends, and coworkers. Look for new connections, and take the time to nurture your relationships.

For long-term success, you need to take care of your mental and physical health. You need enough sleep, healthy food, and regular exercise. Also, make time for activities that help you manage your anxiety and stress levels.

If you fail at something, embrace it and learn from it rather than let it get you down. Failure is part of learning and growing. Don't see failure as a reflection of low worth but as an opportunity to learn and try again.

Find a purpose for your life. Purpose will give your life meaning and direction and you'll be more fulfilled. Identifying your passions and values, and finding ways to incorporate them into your life and work, is essential.

Success can be made up of small victories that eventually build up to a big achievements. We often have to be patient when it comes to achieving our goals. How happy you are could also depend on if you're living the vision you have for your life. It will be difficult to achieve success if you don't have dreams or goals that inspire you.

Being happy will also depend on balancing different factors such as your goals, a positive mindset, supportive relationships in your life, and self-care practices. You can achieve happiness and success by cultivating positive emotions, prioritizing your self-care when needed, and setting achievable goals for yourself.

You could also be more successful if you're happier in life. Joyful people tend to be more productive and creative, and can even have superior problem-solving abilities.

Cheerfulness can also help you develop a positive mindset and outlook, which makes it easier to build resilience and overcome challenges that you may encounter on your road to success.

Happier people usually also have more successful relationships and stronger social connections, which can help you when it comes to achieving your goals.

Creative Success—James McAvoy's Story

The Scottish actor James McAvoy has managed to achieve remarkable creative success, even though he doesn't come from a privileged background like many other British actors.

McAvoy is known for his diverse range of roles in both film and theater. Several factors have contributed to his creative success.

McAvoy has showcased his versatility as an actor by portraying a wide range of characters: from the lovable Mr. Tumnus in *The Chronicles of Narnia* to the complex and tormented Kevin Wendell Crumb in *Split*. His ability to immerse himself in different roles has earned him critical acclaim and a devoted fan base.

The star received formal acting training at the Royal Scottish Academy of Music and Drama (now the Royal Conservatoire of Scotland) and has credited this training with helping him develop his craft. He has admitted to challenging himself by working with directors who push him out of his comfort zone.

The actor has also worked with many respected directors and actors including Danny Boyle, M. Night Shyamalan, and Michael Fassbender. These collaborations helped him learn from the best in the business, which allowed him to refine his own approach to acting.

McAvoy is known for his work ethic and dedication to his craft. He has said in interviews that he takes his roles very seriously and puts in a lot of time and effort to get into character and prepare for his performances.

McAvoy has made bold and creative choices in his career, such as taking on the challenging role of a man with 23 different personalities in *Split* or playing Macbeth and Cyrano de Bergerac in contemporary productions of these plays. These choices have helped him stand out as an actor, and have contributed to his creative success.

Overall, McAvoy's creative success can be attributed to his versatility, training, collaborations, hard work and dedication, and creative choices.

He has established himself as a respected and talented actor, with a long and successful career still ahead of him.

Are My Dreams Worth Anything?

We are always told we should follow our dreams, as this will make our lives happy in the long term. While ambitions can bring a sense of purpose to your life, it's important to pursue them meaningfully. So, how do you decide if it's going to be worth your while to follow your desires?

Before you start pursuing your dreams, think about what you stand to lose in the process. If your dream is something worth having, you're likely going to have to pay a price for it. For example, if you've always wanted to start your own business, you'll have to make sacrifices to reach this goal. For financial security, you may have to give up your full-time job to make your dream come true. While you'll have more freedom if you work for yourself, you'll have very little free time, especially when you initially start your business. Entrepreneurs usually work harder than when they were full-time employees, as they are invested in the success of their businesses.

Therefore, make sure you know what you are letting yourself in for when you start pursuing your dreams. Consider what you're willing to give up to achieve your goals. Can you afford to give up financial security while you pursue a career that is your passion?

Consider that it might also be a lonely road and that everyone won't believe in what you're doing or support you. You might experience self-doubt and plenty of setbacks; but, if you're resilient, you'll be able to keep going. Your dreams might take longer to achieve, or you may have to put your dreams on hold if you run into financial trouble. For example, you may need to look at other ways of earning money, such as working part-time, while still pursuing your intention of running your own business.

To increase your chances of achieving success, clearly define your dream. Create a plan for how you will get there, and set goals

Be optimistic in the pursuit of your dreams. If you find that something isn't working, don't be afraid to change it. Start taking small steps toward achieving your targets. Also, set up a routine that helps you keep track, and don't become distracted from achieving your goals.

Surround yourself with positive people, especially those who are willing to support you when it comes to achieving your dreams. Don't allow yourself to listen to critical people who can't offer you any constructive criticism.

It's important to accept that reaching your objective won't happen overnight. Pursuing your dreams is about the journey, and also what you can learn at every step along the way; it's not only about the final destination.

Finally, even though money is so important in our modern world, following your dreams doesn't need to have anything to do with money. It's important to remember that the value of your dreams isn't the same as your net worth. If you compare yourself financially to others, you're always going to have less money than someone, but you'll possibly have more valuable life experiences and life satisfaction than many others will ever have.

Chasing your dreams could also mean that you might lose money in the short term, but you could even make more money than you ever dreamed of in the long term.

While some don't want to give up financial security to chase their dreams, there is a cost attached to that, as well. For example, if you take the risk to start a new business, you'll often lose money in the short term, but make more money than you could ever fathom in the long term. You may have left a corporate job behind as a communications specialist, but then find you earn much more money as a freelance writer in the long term.

It's important, therefore, to increase the total value of your life, not only your financial value. If living your dream makes you happy, you'll find that your net worth could also increase as a consequence.

Dreams can distract you from the negative events that are happening in your present life. They give you something loftier to aspire to, and can also help you inspire those around you, including your children.

Have you ever stopped to think that your dreams are showing you who you really are? Many people try to "find themselves" and speculate about what their lives mean, while they should rather be paying attention to their goals. Your dreams are part of your life's purpose.

However, we're told in childhood to be realistic in life and to stop fantasizing. We're indoctrinated to stay in our comfort zones, and not go out there and do what we really want to do. Fear holds us back, and when we realize—toward the end of our lives—what we really wanted to do, it's often too late to act on it. Start with personal growth and development at an early age, to get the most out of it. However, if you manage to embrace this mindset later in your life, it's fine too.

Factors That Can Undermine Your Dreams

Low self-esteem can set you back when it comes to achieving your dreams. You may feel like you don't deserve to achieve them and struggle with self-doubt; this will make it extremely difficult to take positive actions toward achieving your dreams.

Self-doubt can weigh you down, as it can make it difficult for you to make decisions and take action. You become stuck in a negative thought cycle, which ends up holding you back. Visualize your success while you work toward something, even if your fantasies seem somewhat unrealistic. It's much more likely that you'll succeed if you have a positive mindset and you believe in yourself.

People often struggle to achieve their dreams when they get stuck in the planning stage. Sometimes, you need to just start working, even if you feel you're not quite ready or you don't have all the skills you're going to need.

You need to have clear goals if you hope to achieve success. Many of us have dreams or ideas we want to achieve, but if we don't have a clear vision or plan, we're just making life difficult for ourselves. We might not achieve our wishes at all, or it might take us a very long time, and we end up learning everything the hard way.

Focus is important too. It is easy to become distracted by social media or other things that also need your attention. However, it's so much harder to reach your goals if you're constantly distracted. The best thing you can do is to take a break when you feel distracted, as this will also increase your productivity in the long term.

Perfectionism and fear of failure could be encouraging you to stay in your comfort zone. You will have to accept the fact that you can't be perfect at all times. Remember that making mistakes offers you a learning experience that can help you to achieve success.

Persistence and resilience are other essential traits of successful people. While talent is important, you can still improve your skills over time with practice. For example, if you're a writer, you'll improve with time, and there are courses you can take to improve your writing skills. However, to do this, you must stay in the game, and keep trying. Resilience, or having a thick skin and a willingness to keep bouncing back, will help you overcome setbacks and deal with difficult clients.

Sometimes, we spend too much time and energy working on something which is never going to be successful. That is why it's also important to know when to let go. This can be difficult, but you'll have much-needed time to work on new opportunities and projects.

If you don't have a learning or growth mentality, you might find it difficult to progress. Reading, education, and travel will give you a deeper insight into the world and help you gain knowledge that will help you achieve your dreams. You need to be open-minded and ask questions about everything that is happening in the world around you. We can't know everything, and there will always be opportunities to learn more.

How to Stop Sabotaging Yourself

When it comes to achieving your goals, you also need to stop sabotaging yourself. Here are some simple strategies that can help you do this.

First, you need to identify your self-sabotaging behavior. Are there certain types of behavior that are getting in the way of you achieving success? These patterns could include procrastination, self-doubt, or negative self-talk. If you recognize the behavior, you can start working on changing it.

When you notice negative thoughts, you need to challenge them. Ask yourself if these thoughts are helpful and even true and replace them with more positive statements if you find they're not.

Make sure that the goals you set for yourself are realistic. Setting impossible goals just makes it easier for you to give up when you fail. You need achievable goals that you can even break up into smaller steps. You also need a plan of action to help you stay on track.

Stop surrounding yourself with people who can only offer unhealthy criticism. You need people who believe in you, as the right support will help you stay motivated.

When you're working toward achieving something, it's easy to forget that you need to pay attention to your health too. If you develop unhealthy habits, such as eating too much junk food or not exercising, you can become mentally and physically exhausted, and end up falling ill, which means it will just take longer for you to achieve your dreams.

It can take time and effort to achieve your dreams. By preventing self-sabotage you can focus on your goals and make faster progress toward living the life you want.

Success Against the Odds—Eminem's Story

World-renowned rapper, Eminem, or Marshall Mathers, had a rough childhood. He grew up in a poor family, had to face poverty and a troubled home life, and was bullied at the various schools he attended. He dropped out of school in the 8th grade to work and support his family.

However, he found his escape in music and rapping at a young age. Even though he was talented and worked hard, he was rejected by many record labels and was severely criticized for his controversial and provocative image and lyrics. He refused to give up and continued to write songs and perform.

By 1997, he'd caught the attention of the producer and rapper, Dr. Dre, who signed him to his record label. Eminem's debut album was released in 1999 and became an instant success. This is after he'd released a failed

YOU MATTER AND YOUR DREAMS ARE VALID

album in 1996 that had sold only 1000 copies. The Slim Shady LP went on to win a Grammy Award and sold around 18 million copies.

After that, Eminem's albums were all commercial and critical successes. Although he still faced personal and addiction struggles, he didn't give up but continued to use his music for self-expression.

In 2022, Eminem was inducted into the Rock and Roll Hall of Fame, and today he is regarded as one of the greatest musicians of all time.

His story can be an inspiration to creative people who are trying to achieve success, in whatever field they may be. Eminem shows us that with perseverance and hard work, it is possible to achieve your dreams, against all odds.

Key Takeaways

- Success can mean different things to different people and you need to define what it means to you.
- Success doesn't necessarily involve money, titles, and fame.
- It's never too late in your life to pursue your true passion.
- It is possible to achieve success by doing something you enjoy.
- There are benefits to pursuing success slightly later in life, as you will have skills, knowledge, and maturity that you can use in different fields.
- Stan Lee is a good example of someone who only achieved success slightly later in his life, as he only became famous for his comic books when he was already in his forties.
- Low self-esteem can be a barrier when it comes to achieving success, as you'll probably feel like you don't deserve success.

- There are different types of success, namely academic, career, financial, personal, and creative success.
- Spiritual success might also become increasingly popular with people especially as they get older.
- If you fail at something, don't let that stop you from achieving success. See failure as a learning opportunity and keep going.
- Happy people can be more productive and creative, which boosts their problem-solving abilities.
- Before you start pursuing your dreams, you also need to think about what you stand to lose in the process.
- There is always a price to pay for dreams that are worth achieving. For example, if you want to start a business, you might have to give up a steady income from your full-time job.
- You should also realize that not everyone will support you when it comes to achieving your dreams. Some people might be extremely critical which will make you doubt yourself. Avoid them.
- Achieving your dreams won't happen overnight, and the process is part of the journey.
- Dreams can distract you from negative events that are happening in your present life. They give you something to aspire you, even if you're having problems in your life currently, such as financial challenges.
- Some people struggle to achieve their dreams when they get stuck in the planning stage. Sometimes you just have to start, even if it feels like you're not quite ready.

- You also need clear goals and focus to achieve success.
- Persistence and resilience are important when it comes to achieving success.
- You need to identify and stop self-sabotaging behavior.
- It's vital to take care of your health while pursuing your goals.

Practical Activity—Create Your Own Definition of Success

To achieve the success that is meaningful to you, you first need to define what type of success means something to you, and excites you. While other people might expect you to achieve certain things, you will only really see yourself as successful, if you achieve something truly important to you.

On a piece of paper or in your journal, answer the following questions. This will help you take your first steps on the journey to define what success means to you.

- Define, in as much detail as possible, what success means to you. Do you see it as achieving at work, starting a successful business, or having financial freedom, or is it more about personal happiness?
- How do you see your life as being different after you achieve success? Will you have more money to spend or move somewhere else? Will you look at yourself in a different light, as being more worthwhile than before?

Don't spend too much time thinking about what success means to you, or looking for the perfect idea. Many people wait for that special idea and then never start, partially because they also lack confidence. Sometimes you just need to take the leap and start, even if you're scared to do so.

It's often not possible to figure out every single detail before you start something. You may feel that you don't know enough or that the lack of knowledge is going to cause you to fail. Think about what you would do if fear wasn't holding you back and how hard you would push to achieve even more success. What goals would you want to achieve if you weren't afraid?

CHAPTER 3:
OVERCOMING NEGATIVITY THE FIRST STEPS

Overcoming negativity is the first step you need to take when it comes to finding happiness.

As humans, we're more likely to be affected by negative experiences and events than by positive ones. This is a result of the brain's tendency to give more attention to unpleasant experiences.

This negativity bias is said to be part of the survival mechanism of early humans, as negative events had more significant consequences for survival and safety. This bias is not so useful today, as it can lead to anxiety and depression.

How Negativity Starts and Grows

Negative emotions can influence how we make decisions, behave, and interact with others. Negativity can influence the way you make decisions. If you are too focused on potentially unfavorable outcomes, you could make poor decisions.

People who make decisions based on negativity are often also averse to loss.

Cognitive Distortions That Make for Negativity

The negativity bias and loss aversion are related cognitive biases that can influence behavior and decision-making.

The problem with cognitive distortions is that they cause inaccurate thinking and we can convince ourselves of untrue things.

A cognitive bias is a diversion from objective thinking which happens when our brain is processing information. This could lead to irrational decisions, beliefs, and behavior. Cognitive biases were useful in times and situations where quick decisions had to be taken—for example, when survival was at stake. However, they can become a problem if decisions are made based on inaccurate information.

Both negativity bias and loss aversion are thought to be evolutionary adaptations that helped our ancestors survive in harsh and unpredictable environments. Focusing on potential threats and avoiding losses helped them avoid danger and stay alive. However, in modern society, these biases can lead to over-cautiousness, anxiety, and missed opportunities.

While the negativity bias might once have been necessary for our survival, this bias now manifests in ways that can be bad for our mental health; we might obsess about negative feedback or criticism, and make our decisions based on fear of the risks of a situation, rather than the benefits.

If you're averse to loss, you feel more strongly about forfeiting something than gaining something. This could also lead to irrational decisions–for example, if you're unwilling to take a risk where you could potentially gain big because you are too afraid of the possibility of losses.

Confirmation Bias

Confirmation bias is our brain's natural tendency to filter out information that doesn't agree with our beliefs and worldviews.

People with a strong confirmation bias tend to interpret new information in a way that will confirm their existing attitudes and beliefs. They might ignore information that goes against their beliefs, which could lead to biased decision-making.

People will give information that supports their beliefs more often than that which contradicts their beliefs. This type of bias can also lead to group polarization. People are more likely to interact with and also surround themselves with, like-minded people who share their beliefs and opinions. When people are encircled by others who share their beliefs, they're more likely to be extreme and dismissive when it comes to their views.

Confirmation bias can also cause people to make poor choices that lead to negative outcomes and even conflict, as people often become defensive when their beliefs are challenged.

You should strive to overcome confirmation bias by being open-minded and listening to diverse opinions and perspectives. Always be willing to have your beliefs challenged and consider alternative viewpoints. If you actively work to counteract this bias, you'll be able to make better decisions.

Black-and-White Thinking

Black-and-white thinking, or all-or-nothing thinking, involves seeing the world in an extreme and polarized way. The danger with this type of reasoning is that you could oversimplify complex situations if your perspective is too narrow and rigid.

If you engage in this type of thinking, you usually see people, events, and situations in binary terms. You either see a situation as being good or bad, a success or failure, or even right or wrong—with nothing in between.

It could affect your self-love negatively if you apply this type of thinking to yourself, and see yourself as either good or bad at things, without recognizing and understanding your strengths and weaknesses.

If you're a black-and-white thinker, it could have negative consequences for your mental health, your relationships with others, and your decision-making abilities. It could also result in a lack of adaptability, intolerance, and difficulty in managing emotions. For example, you might struggle to consider alternative viewpoints, which could cause conflicts and misunderstandings in your relationships.

It's possible to overcome this type of cognitive distortion by practicing mindfulness, and by becoming aware of your thoughts and emotions. It will also help you to try to see situations from different perspectives. You will have to accept that there aren't always clear-cut solutions to every challenge.

Overgeneralization

If you overgeneralize, you tend to draw conclusions based on very limited or insufficient evidence. This could cause inaccurate beliefs about yourself and the world around you.

For example, if you've been turned down for several jobs, you may start to feel that you're not good enough, or efficient enough, to get the positions that you want—even if there is no evidence that this is true.

Another common overgeneralization is when someone has a negative experience with a member of a certain group, and then assumes that all members of that group are the same.

Overgeneralization can be bad for your mental health, as it can lead to social anxiety and low self-esteem. It can also lead to prejudice against others and unfair discrimination. If you want to overcome overgeneralization, you need to challenge your beliefs by looking for evidence that will contradict them.

Personalization

Personalization is a tendency to take everything personally, even though it may not have anything to do with you. This can lead to a lot of guilt, shame, and even anxiety. This cognitive distortion could cause us to behave in ways that could be harmful to ourselves or others.

Personalization also happens when people assume they're responsible for everything happening around them, even things or situations that aren't within their control. People who have this mindset often end up feeling ashamed or guilty, even if there's no evidence to support these beliefs. For example, if a potential romantic partner doesn't return their interest, they may think something is wrong with them and that they will never find a partner.

People who tend to personalize everything usually also don't deal well with feedback; even constructive criticism. They may see it as a personal attack, and not as a useful exercise that can help them improve their work.

The best way to combat personalization is to, again, challenge the thoughts when they arise. Ask yourself if there is any evidence to support your beliefs, and consider other factors that could be contributing to it, rather than automatically assuming you're responsible.

Filtering

Filtering involves focusing on only the negative aspects while ignoring the positive. This could cause a distorted view of reality, and we might feel more negative emotions that can impact behavior and relationships.

People who engage in this cognitive distortion may dwell on negative experiences and events, even when there are positive aspects present.

For example, this could apply to someone who, in general, receives positive feedback on a project they've completed; but, only focuses on the minor negative feedback they receive, on where they can make improvements. They could turn a minor criticism into a huge setback.

There are ways to overcome filtering, such as making lists of the positive aspects of a situation or event and choosing to focus on those, rather than the negative aspects. It can be helpful to consider detrimental events as learning opportunities.

Availability Bias

This cognitive bias refers to our tendency to overestimate the likelihood that something will happen because the type of event is easily remembered or recalled. The perception of reality is distorted, as more emotionally charged or vivid events are more likely to be remembered than those that are less so.

For example, we could overestimate the chances of a certain crime happening close to us if we've recently heard about it on the news, even if the actual crime rate is fairly low.

The availability bias can also influence decision-making, as we could tend to make decisions based on readily available information, rather than looking at a situation more comprehensively. This could even lead to irrational behavior since all evidence isn't considered and the available information is often emotionally charged.

You can counteract this bias by looking for more objective sources of information and not only relying on your memories and experiences. You also need to be aware of the impact that your emotions and experiences can have on your decision-making and perceptions. It's important to make a conscious effort to consider all available information before you finally make a decision.

Illusory Correlation

Illusory correlation refers to a tendency to see a relationship that doesn't exist or to overestimate the strength of a relationship. This type of bias could lead to incorrect beliefs about causality which could, in turn, result in people creating inaccurate judgments and making the wrong decisions.

For example, this way of thinking could also lead to stereotyping and inaccurate conclusions such as if colleagues at a workplace think that a female manager won't be successful because she would be too emotional.

This bias could also lead to discriminatory behavior—for example, a healthcare provider who provides suboptimal care to overweight patients who believes their main problem to be that they're simply obese, and they don't consider sending the patient for tests to investigate possible other reasons for their ill health.

When it comes to combating this bias, it's important not to make decisions based on incomplete or subjective information. All available evidence should be considered before making a decision. You should also be willing, and able, to change your beliefs in the face of new evidence, and you shouldn't cling to beliefs that could be based on illusory correlations.

Discovering the Root Causes of Your Negativity

It's essential to discover the root causes of your negativity, as this will also help you improve your overall well-being, and overcome these types of emotions.

Firstly, you need to be able to identify your negative thoughts and emotions. When you feel upset, take some time to think about what triggered those emotions.

Your beliefs and values can also be playing a role in your behavior and emotions. You need to reflect on your values and beliefs from time to time, and consider if they're serving you or if they are just holding you back.

If you tend to compare yourself to others, you need to be aware that this type of behavior can trigger negative emotions. Many of us have developed a habit of comparing ourselves to other people's social media feeds. It's especially important to note that most people only share the highlights of their lives on social media, and not the challenges they had to overcome and the depressing moments. There's never a good reason to compare yourself with others; rather, you should focus on your personal growth and becoming the best version of yourself that you can be.

Consider how your past experiences could be contributing to your current negativity. If you've experienced trauma, or have had other difficult experiences, they could have caused long-term emotional scarring.

Your present situation could be contributing to the negative emotions that you're currently experiencing. These could be relationship difficulties or career stress. Consider whether there are ways you can improve your current way of life.

Underestimating your abilities could also be contributing to your negativity.

If you're struggling to identify the root cause of your negativity, or you can't deal with it on your own, you may need to see a therapist or counselor. They could help you explore your negative emotions, and help you develop strategies to overcome these thought patterns.

When you fail at something, it just means you need to practice more or work harder. If you see yourself as less competent than you are, you just lower your self-esteem, which will make you doubt yourself in everything you do. Consider your attitude when you have to face challenges. If it's too easy for you to come up with excuses, you need to work on your attitude.

You will also tend to be more negative if you don't fully believe you're in charge of your life. You need to accept that you're in charge of your destiny and that your actions will make a difference when it comes to achieving your goals and improving your life. It will be easier to make the necessary changes if you start believing in yourself.

Your environment, and the people you associate with, also have an impact on your mindset. If you are always surrounded by negative people, you'll also start spreading the same negativity to others. Most positive people are the way they are because they separate themselves from negative energy.

Inner Critic Reworking (How to Turn the Voice in Your Head into a Friend)

A negative inner critic can demoralize you, and influence how you feel and behave. However, there are things you can do to reframe your negative thoughts.

What is this inner critic and where does it come from?

The inner critic is that nagging voice in your head that keeps telling you that you're not good enough. It often develops as a result of how we were treated by our caregivers in early childhood. If you had overbearing, overly critical, or abusive parents, you might find it difficult to develop a positive inner voice in adulthood.

Unfortunately, we tend to adopt this criticism and develop a very critical inner voice that can make life difficult for us as we get older. This constant self-criticism can cause mental health problems, such as anxiety and depression.

Our inner critic makes us believe that whatever goes wrong is our fault. Your inner critic may tell you that you're fat, ugly, or stupid and that you don't deserve to get something.

The Negative Impact of the Inner Critic

The inner critic can damage your self-esteem and your ability to appreciate yourself. A repeated negative thought cycle can make you feel helpless and hopeless, and will only diminish your motivation.

There are things you can do to change your inner critic into a kinder voice. It's possible to distance yourself from negative messages.

First of all, you need to be able to identify when this voice is speaking to you. Also, analyze the language it uses and think about how it makes you feel. When your inner critic starts to speak to you, challenge its negative statements. Ask yourself if there is any evidence to support them. Another way of dealing with these thoughts is to accept them, and then let them go and move on.

You could also try to reframe your thoughts more positively. For instance, instead of straightaway thinking that you can't do something, tell yourself that you're willing to give it a try or that you are willing to learn.

It's also important to practice being kind to yourself and treat yourself like you would treat a good friend or family member who has gone through a tough time. Be empathetic toward your thoughts and feelings. For example, if you have had a bad accident and you've just gone back to work recently, give yourself time to adjust and heal. You won't be able to immediately start functioning at work at the same level as before your accident. You may also be suffering from PTSD, and you could need therapy or further treatment.

Don't let your inner critic stop you from completing the actions that you intend to take. You could talk to a friend or therapist about your inner critic, and they could support you and help you gain perspective on your situation.

Reframing Your Negative Thoughts

Reframing refers to the process of changing the way a situation or problem is perceived or understood, to shift the focus, alter the context, or provide a different perspective. It involves looking at a situation from a different angle, or in a new light, to uncover new opportunities or solutions that were not previously apparent.

It can be a powerful tool for problem-solving, communication, and personal growth—as it allows you to break free from old patterns of thinking and behavior, and open yourself up to new possibilities. It can also help you to develop a more positive way of thinking when you reframe your negative thoughts.

Reframing is a powerful technique that can help you shift your perspective and think more positively. When you reframe a situation, you focus on the positive aspects instead of the negative ones. Thus, if you're facing a challenging situation at work, instead of focusing on the problem, you can focus on the opportunity to learn something new or improve your skills. If you fail at doing something, see what you can learn from the situation, and how you can prevent a similar failure in the future.

Reassessing allows you to change the way you interpret a situation. For example, if you lose a bicycle race for which you have been training a long time, don't see it as losing, but think about all the exercise you got as part of your practice and how much you learned about the sport, and also bicycles, while preparing for this race. You can always participate in other races in the future, and your experience will help you do better the next time you participate.

This technique can also help you find the silver lining in any situation. For instance, if a relationship ends, it might give you the chance to focus more on yourself and work on your goals and dreams, such as studying for a higher degree or traveling.

Reframing allows you to shift your perspective and look at a situation from a different angle. For example, if you're stuck in traffic, instead of becoming frustrated, you can use the time to listen to music or a podcast and relax.

Cultivate gratitude by focusing on the positive aspects of your life. For example, instead of focusing on what you don't have, you can focus on what you do have and be grateful for it.

Overall, reframing can help you think more positively by allowing you to focus on the bright side of a situation, find the silver lining, shift your perspective, and cultivate gratitude. You can develop a more positive outlook on life by developing this attitude.

Emma Stone's Story—Dealing With Her Inner Critic

One celebrity who has spoken openly about dealing with their inner critic is actress Emma Stone, who appeared in the movie *Crazy, Stupid, Love*.

Stone said that she developed a positive mindset, and didn't dwell on the negative aspects of her career. The actress also said that she tries to cultivate gratitude and appreciation for what she has already achieved in her life.

The actress has also learned to accept imperfection, and not be too hard on herself when things don't go as planned. She tries to be kind and forgiving towards herself, even when she makes mistakes.

Stone credits her supportive family and friends who have helped her to accept her imperfections.

Key Takeaways

- You need to overcome your negativity first before you can find true happiness.
- Human beings tend to be more affected by negative experiences than positive ones. This is known as the negativity bias and is thought to have been part of early humans' survival mechanisms.
- The negativity bias is not useful in modern times, as it can cause anxiety and depression.
- Negative emotions can influence how we behave, make decisions, and interact with others.
- A cognitive bias is a diversion from objective thinking which happens when our brains are processing information.
- Cognitive distortions can cause inaccurate thinking, and we can convince ourselves of things that aren't true. It could lead to irrational decisions and behavior.
- The cognitive biases can include confirmation bias, black-and-white thinking, overgeneralization, personalization, filtering, availability bias, and illusory correlation.
- You need to discover the root cause of your negativity to improve your overall well-being.

- Past experiences could be contributing to your current negativity. Childhood trauma could cause long-lasting negativity.
- Underestimating your abilities could contribute to your negativity.
- If you're struggling to identify the root cause of your negativity, you may need the help of a therapist or counselor.
- The inner critic in your head is the negative voice that tells you that you're not good enough.
- The inner critic makes us believe that whatever goes wrong is our fault.
- You can reframe your thoughts and turn your inner critic into a kinder voice.

Worksheet: Overcoming Negative Thinking

Negative thoughts can significantly impact your mental health and overall well-being. This worksheet is designed to help you identify and overcome negative thinking patterns.

Instructions

Take some time to think about the questions and exercises below. You can write the answers in your journal. You could also type them on an electronic device if you prefer to keep your journal on your computer or handheld device.

OVERCOMING NEGATIVITY THE FIRST STEPS

Identify negative thinking patterns

> - What negative thoughts have you experienced lately?
> - Do you know what triggers your negative thoughts?
> - Are there specific situations or people that tend to trigger negative thoughts?

Challenge negative thoughts

Take one of the negative thoughts you identified and challenge it with evidence. Ask yourself if there is any evidence to support this thought, or if it is just a baseless assumption. You can write your answers below, or write them down in your journal.

Negative thought:

_____

_____

Evidence to support this thought:

_____

_____

Evidence against this thought:

_____

_____

Think of an alternative explanation for the situation that led to the negative thought. You can write down your answers below, or write the answers in your journal.

Negative thought:

_____
_____

Alternative explanation:

_____
_____

Practice Positive Self-Talk

Write down three positive affirmations that you can use to replace negative thoughts.

1. _____
2. _____
3. _____

When you notice a negative thought creeping in, replace it with one of the positive affirmations you wrote down. Write down the situation and the positive affirmation you used.

Situation:

_____
_____

Positive affirmation used:

_____
_____

Take Action

Identify one action you can take to improve the situation that led to the negative thought. Write the answer below or in your journal.

Action:

_____

_____

Schedule a time to take this action, and write down the date and time below.

Date and time:

_____

Conclusion

It can take time to overcome negative thinking, but you can change your thinking patterns and improve your overall wellness. Use this worksheet as a tool to help you identify and challenge negative thoughts, practice positive self-talk, and take action to improve your situation.

Worksheet: Dealing with Your Inner Critic

Your inner critic can be a harsh voice that criticizes your every move and causes you to doubt yourself. This can result in low self-esteem, a lack of self-love, and even mental health problems. This worksheet is designed to help you identify and deal with your inner critic.

Instructions

Take some time to think about the questions and exercises below. Write the answers in your journal, so that you can keep track of them. You could

Identify Your Inner Critic

> - What negative things does your inner critic say to you?
> - When does your inner critic tend to be active? (When you make a mistake? During other stressful times?)
> - How does this inner critic make you feel?

Challenge Your Inner Critic

Take one of the negative statements your inner critic says to you, and challenge it with evidence. Is there any evidence to support this statement, or is this assumption baseless? Write your findings below or in your journal.

Inner critic statement:

_____

Evidence to support the statement:

_____

Evidence against the statement:

_____

Come up with a more balanced and realistic statement to replace the negative statement. Write your new statement down below.

Negative statement:

_____

Balanced statement:

_____

Practice Self-Compassion

Write down three kind and supportive statements you can say to yourself when your inner critic shows up—for example, "I can learn from my mistakes and do better next time," or "I am doing the best I can."

_____

_____

_____

_____

Take Action

Identify one action you can take to challenge your inner critic and build your self-confidence. Write down the action below, or in your electronic journal.

Action:

_____

_____

Conclusion

It can be challenging to deal with your inner critic. However, with practice, you can learn to recognize and challenge your negative thoughts, which will help you build your self-confidence. Use this worksheet to challenge your inner critic and build your self-confidence.

CHAPTER 4:
LOW SELF-ESTEEM LEADS TO SELF-NEGLECT

Low self-esteem and self-neglect can contribute to a co-dependent lifestyle. Someone with low self-esteem will struggle to take care of themselves and look after their own needs. They might not feel worthy to receive support and care from others.

People with these tendencies could easily become involved in codependent relationships. They will then put all their energy into taking care of their partner and neglect their own needs.

This type of behavior creates a cycle of dependence where the co-dependent person becomes increasingly dependent on their partner for support and validation.

If someone wants to break free from a codependent lifestyle, this will involve addressing both the low self-esteem and self-neglect that are part of the problem. First, a more positive self-image needs to be created, and self-care and self-compassion also need to be practiced.

What Is Self-Neglect?

Self-neglect happens when someone can't or won't take care of their basic physical, emotional, and social needs. Vulnerable older adults who live alone might neglect themselves; but, others—such as individuals who struggle with mental health or addiction issues—could also suffer from self-neglect.

Self-neglect can take many different forms, but it's often easy to recognize them. Some people may start neglecting their hygiene, while others don't drink or eat enough, or don't seek medical treatment when they need it. Household tasks or the paying of bills could also be neglected. Additionally, some people could withdraw socially.

Self-neglect could have serious consequences when it comes to health, and also overall well-being. Someone who struggles with self-neglect should, first of all, receive medical care and therapy to address any underlying issues.

Is Self-Neglect Caused by Low Self-Esteem?

Self-neglect is a complex issue that can be caused by different factors, including low self-esteem. It could also be caused by physical and mental health conditions, financial difficulties, substance abuse, or cognitive decline.

However, low self-esteem is the major contributing factor to self-neglect, as people who suffer from it possibly do not see the value in taking care of themselves and might not prioritize self-care activities.

Their behavior could also be self-destructive, and their negative self-talk might cause their self-esteem to become even worse and could reinforce their self-neglect.

Low self-esteem can lead to self-neglect in several ways:

> **Lack of self-care:** When people have low self-esteem, they often feel unworthy, and may feel like they don't deserve self-care. This can cause them to neglect their physical, emotional, and mental health needs. For instance, they may not eat enough healthy food, don't get enough sleep, or don't get medical help when they need it. All these neglectful actions will make their self-esteem even worse in the long term.

> **Negative self-talk:** People with low self-esteem often engage in negative self-talk, which could cause them to feel helpless and hopeless. They could start to believe that they're incapable of making meaningful positive changes to their lives, which could also cause them to lose motivation when it comes to taking care of themselves. They may also believe everything negative that has happened to them is their fault, and that they deserve it.

> **Avoidance:** People with low self-esteem may avoid social situations, or activities they enjoy, because they feel they are not good enough or fear being judged. This can lead to isolation and even imposter syndrome—where they believe that, even though they are high achievers, they are worthless frauds who will be found out by others.

> **Substance abuse:** People with low self-esteem could also turn to drug or alcohol abuse to cope with their negative feelings. This could make their self-neglect worse and lead to even more health problems.

How Low Self-Esteem Breeds Unhappiness

Low self-esteem can lead to unhappiness since individuals with low self-esteem often have negative beliefs about themselves, what they can do, and what they are worth as people. They can feel inadequate, insecure, and unhappy with themselves because of this.

Low self-confidence can also lead to a lack of motivation to pursue goals. This could cause people to feel unfulfilled in their personal or career lives, which could cause further unhappiness.

Furthermore, low self-esteem could cause negative relationships with others. When people don't value and love themselves, it will be difficult for them to see that others value them or their opinions. This could lead to loneliness and a lack of meaningful connections with others.

If you can improve your self-esteem, you'll find that your overall happiness and well-being will also improve.

How Low Self-Esteem Can Cause Unhappiness

Low self-esteem can cause unhappiness in our lives in several different ways:

- ➢ It can cause negative self-talk, which means we will constantly be criticizing ourselves and our abilities. This could cause us to feel worthless and see ourselves as failures.
- ➢ Low self-esteem could also cause us to doubt our abilities, which will undermine our confidence and motivation, leading to further unhappiness.
- ➢ People with low self-esteem could find it difficult to form and maintain healthy and meaningful relationships. They could

> avoid social situations, as they feel unworthy of receiving affection from others, which will lead to increasing social isolation and loneliness.
>
> ➢ Someone with low self-esteem might not feel it's possible to achieve their goals, which could cause them to become unfulfilled and unhappy. They could also develop mental health conditions, such as depression and anxiety.

What Is Imposter Syndrome?

A person who suffers from imposter syndrome doubts their accomplishments and fears that they will eventually be exposed as a fraud. Usually, people who suffer from this condition are high achievers, and there is plenty of evidence that they're not the failures they see themselves as being. However, they often believe their success is simply the result of good luck, and not because of their superior abilities or hard work.

They feel like "imposters" in the sense that they think they're pretending to be someone who they aren't—such as smart and talented high achievers.

Imposter syndrome is bad for your mental health and overall well-being, as it could cause anxiety and depression, as well as self-sabotage, and people may start to avoid new challenges and opportunities.

Low Self-Esteem and Imposter Syndrome

Low self-esteem is one of the main contributing factors to imposter syndrome. People with low self-esteem have negative beliefs about themselves and their abilities, and they don't think they deserve success.

Low self-esteem can also contribute to a lack of self-confidence, which can make it difficult to accept praise or recognition for one's accomplishments. This can reinforce feelings of imposter syndrome, as the person may feel like they are deceiving others by accepting praise for something they don't feel they deserve.

It is important to address and manage imposter syndrome, which can be done through therapy, self-reflection, and self-care practices such as positive self-talk and self-compassion. Building self-esteem and acknowledging one's strengths and accomplishments can also help alleviate this syndrome and improve mental health in general.

How Low Self-Esteem Encourages Failure

Low self-esteem and failure can be closely linked, as a low self-esteem can contribute to a lack of confidence, motivation, and resilience—all of which can increase the likelihood of failure.

If you have low self-esteem, you could believe that you're not capable or worthy of achieving your goals. This negative self-talk can lead to a lack of confidence and motivation to try, which can result in failure. In addition, people with low self-esteem may be more likely to give up easily or avoid challenges, which can limit their opportunities for success.

Furthermore, when someone experiences failure, it can reinforce their negative beliefs about themselves and lead to a further decline in self-esteem. This negative cycle can create a self-fulfilling prophecy, where the person's low self-esteem leads to failure, which then reinforces their negative beliefs and leads to further defeat.

However, it's important to note that failure is a natural part of the learning process, and everyone experiences it at some point in their lives. The key is to develop a growth mindset, which emphasizes learning and improvement rather than success or failure. By focusing on learning from failures and mistakes, rather than seeing them as a reflection of one's worth or abilities, people with low self-esteem can build resilience and confidence over time.

Overall, low self-esteem can contribute to failure, but it is possible to break the negative cycle by developing a growth mindset and seeking support from others when needed.

Low self-esteem can encourage failure in several ways. When someone has low self-esteem, they may have negative beliefs about their abilities, worth, and potential. These beliefs can lead to a lack of confidence, motivation, and persistence—making it more difficult to achieve their goals.

People with low self-esteem are more inclined to feel a failure as it confirms their negative views and beliefs about themselves. This could cause them to avoid taking risks and will make it difficult for them to face challenges. This means opportunities for success are limited.

People with low self-esteem usually have negative self-talk, which creates a vicious cycle of believing they will fail, which then further undermines their confidence and makes them nervous and more likely to fail. This makes it difficult for them to ever reach their full potential.

This type of negative thinking also encourages self-sabotaging behavior, such as procrastination, which will further limit someone's chances of achieving success

If you have low self-esteem, you may also be struggling with a lack of resilience, which will make it even more difficult to bounce back from challenges. A lack of resilience also leads to a lack of perseverance.

If you feel that your self-esteem is low and holding you back from achieving happiness and success, you need to address the issues. Seek help from a mental health professional, if you feel the need to do so.

LOW SELF-ESTEEM LEADS TO SELF-NEGLECT

Being a Pushover Is Not Attractive

In colloquial language, a "pushover" is someone who is easily influenced, persuaded, or manipulated. It is used to describe someone who is weak-willed, lacks confidence, and can be easily taken advantage of by others.

The term "pushover" is often used to describe someone who is overly accommodating, always saying *yes* to the demands of others, and unable to stand up for themselves. This can lead to the person being manipulated and may result in them being exploited or mistreated.

Overall, being a pushover is generally considered a negative trait as it can lead to a lack of assertiveness, self-esteem, and personal boundaries. However, it's possible to develop the skills and confidence to set boundaries and stand up for yourself.

Signs You're a Pushover

The following could be signs that you're a pushover:

- You find it difficult to say "no" to others, and you often take on more work than you're able to handle.
- You allow others to cross your personal boundaries and invade your personal space or waste your time, without any regard for your preferences.
- You always put the needs and interests of others ahead of your own.
- You avoid confrontation and prefer to keep the peace, even if you have to sacrifice your own needs.
- You find it difficult to express your thoughts and feelings, especially if they are different from those of other people.

> You're constantly looking for approval from other people, and you feel anxious or stressed when you don't receive it.
> You feel like you don't have control over your own life, and others are making decisions for you.

How to Stop Being a Pushover

Don't worry if you're struggling with being a people pleaser and a pushover. There are things you can do to overcome these tendencies.

First of all, you need to identify your values, what is important in your life, and what you stand for. Knowledge like this will help you create boundaries and prioritize your own needs. You need to communicate your boundaries clearly to others to protect your time, space, and energy.

You need to develop, and practice, the skill of saying "no" to others. You can start practicing by saying "no" to small things that don't align with your values or what you don't feel like doing. This skill will also help you build your confidence, and you'll find that you become more assertive.

It's important to learn good communication skills, which can also help you a great deal when it comes to expressing your thoughts and feelings clearly and respectfully. This can help you not to become resentful and bottle up your emotions.

You need to work on developing your self-confidence by focusing on your strengths and accomplishments. When you are confident, you'll be much more comfortable standing up for yourself and prioritizing your needs.

You need to take responsibility for your life and recognize that you're in control of the decisions you make. As an adult, others shouldn't be making your decisions, or influencing those decisions.

If you need support, talk to your friends and family, and even look for a therapist or a coach. Support will help you stay motivated, and you'll receive guidance and encouragement.

How to Say "No"

If you want to stop being a pushover, one of the most important skills you will need is the ability to say "no" to others. Saying "no" can be difficult, especially if you're used to being a people pleaser or a pushover.

Here are some tips to help you say "no" confidently and respectfully:

- When saying "no," be direct and clear in your language. Don't feel that you have to make excuses or give reasons. Nobody has the right to feel that you have to do things for them.
- Use "I" statements to express your needs and preferences. For example, say, "I'm not comfortable with that" instead of "You're making me uncomfortable."
- It can be helpful to provide a brief explanation for why you're saying "no," but keep it simple and to the point. For example, "I will be busy" or "I have another appointment."
- If possible, offer an alternative solution that meets both your needs and those of the other person. For example, "I can't make it to dinner tonight, but how about we meet for lunch next week?"
- It's okay to express regret or empathy, but don't apologize excessively or make it seem like you're in the wrong for saying "no."
- Practicing saying "no" in low-stakes situations, such as declining an invitation to a social event, can help you build your confidence.

> Remember that saying "no" is not a negative thing. It's important to prioritize your own needs and set healthy boundaries in your personal and professional life.

How to Say "No" to Self-Neglect and Codependency

Codependency is a behavioral condition in which an individual tends to depend excessively on others for their emotional and psychological well-being, often to the detriment of their own needs and desires.

The following are signs that you could be codependent:

> You find it difficult to set boundaries: Co-dependents often have difficulty setting boundaries and saying *no* to others, which can lead to overcommitment and neglect of their own needs.

> You have low self-esteem: Codependents often have a low sense of self-worth and may rely on others for validation and approval.

> You need to control others: Codependents may feel the need to control or micromanage others in an attempt to feel needed or important.

> Your communication skills aren't that well-developed; Codependents may struggle with healthily expressing their needs and emotions, leading to misunderstandings and conflict in relationships.

> You have a fear that you will be abandoned: Codependents may have a deep-seated fear of being abandoned or rejected by others, leading them to cling to relationships, even if they are unhealthy.

Emotional Neglect and People-Pleasing Behavior

Emotional neglect can lead to people-pleasing behavior in several ways. You may have been emotionally neglected during childhood if your caregivers didn't give you enough emotional support, or if they didn't pay attention to your emotional needs.

Over time, you may have come to believe your emotional needs aren't valid or important. This could have led you to believe that you must prioritize others' emotional needs over your own, to feel loved and valued.

People who have experienced emotional neglect may develop a pattern of accommodating behavior to feel accepted and loved by others. They may go out of their way to meet others' needs and expectations, even at the expense of their own emotional well-being.

This can lead to a cycle of seeking validation and approval from others, rather than developing a strong sense of self-worth and self-validation.

Overcoming Codependency

It's possible to overcome codependent behavior with time and commitment. The first step is to recognize your codependent behavior. Try to determine how you rely on others for your self-worth.

You need to pay close attention to your actions and thoughts in relationships and notice when you start to act codependently.

You need to find out what is making you behave in this way. Codependent behavior is often the result of childhood experiences of neglect, abuse, or instability.

Reflect on your past experiences and how they may have contributed to your codependent behavior.

It's also important to take care of your own physical, emotional, and mental needs. You need to be able to set boundaries and prioritize your well-being.

Develop a support network of family and friends who can support your personal growth and recovery.

Work on developing assertive communication skills, as this will help you express your needs and desires in relationships.

If you feel you need help with underlying issues, consider looking for professional help. A good therapist can help you develop strategies to overcome codependency. Remember that it's a process that will take time and effort and that you should be patient with yourself.

Overcoming Codependency—Jennifer Lopez's Story

Popular actress and singer Jennifer Lopez has openly talked about overcoming an unhealthy and codependent relationship in her memoir.

Lopez was in a relationship with musician Marc Anthony for ten years, and they have two children together. She describes their relationship as being based on codependency, where they relied on each other for validation and support, even when they weren't happy together.

In the book, Lopez talks about how she sought therapy and learned to set boundaries in her relationships. She also discusses the importance of self-love and learning to be happy on her own, rather than depending on others for her happiness.

Lopez said she was ultimately able to break free from her co-dependent relationship with Anthony and move on to a healthier, more fulfilling life. Her story can inspire others who are struggling to free themselves from codependent relationships.

LOW SELF-ESTEEM LEADS TO SELF-NEGLECT

Key Takeaways

- Low self-esteem and self-neglect can contribute to a codependent lifestyle.
- Someone with low self-esteem may struggle to take care of themselves and look after their own needs.
- Self-neglect happens when someone can't take care of their basic needs.
- Self-neglect can have serious consequences when it comes to health and overall well-being.
- Someone who struggles with self-neglect should, first of all, receive medical care to deal with any underlying issues.
- Low self-esteem can lead to unhappiness, as people with low self-esteem often have negative beliefs about themselves.
- Low self-esteem could cause you to doubt your abilities.
- Someone who suffers from imposter syndrome will doubt their accomplishments and fear that they will eventually be exposed as a fraud.
- Low self-esteem is the main contributing factor to imposter syndrome.
- It's vital to realize failure is an important part of the learning process, and that everyone experiences it in their life, at some point.
- Learning good communication skills can help you to not be a people pleaser or "pushover."

Worksheet: Overcoming Low Self-Esteem

Instructions

This worksheet aims to help you understand the causes of your low self-esteem and to overcome them. Answer the questions below honestly and thoughtfully. Write your answers down to give yourself some time to reflect on them.

Questions

- Think about some negative beliefs you hold about yourself and write them down.
- Can you determine where these beliefs come from? Could they have developed in your childhood, and be based on messages you received from your caretakers?
- How do these negative beliefs affect your life? Have they been holding you back from pursuing your goals? Do you feel depressed or anxious?
- Name your positive qualities and strengths.
- Consider ways in which you can start focusing on your positive qualities and strengths, instead of your negative beliefs.
- Think of ways in which you can challenge and reframe your negative thoughts and beliefs. Also, write down the evidence you have to contradict these beliefs.
- How can you practice self-compassion and self-care to improve your self-esteem?

LOW SELF-ESTEEM LEADS TO SELF-NEGLECT

> ➢ Name some healthy ways you can cope with negative thoughts and feelings about yourself.

> ➢ Who can you reach out to for support when you are struggling with low self-esteem? Do you have a solid support network of family and friends?

> ➢ What steps can you take to improve your self-esteem?

Think about your answers, and write down any additional insights you gained while you were doing the exercise. Remember that it will take time and effort to overcome your low self-esteem.

CHAPTER 5:
FORGIVE THE PAST, FORGIVE YOURSELF

Unforgiveness and unhappiness are often closely related. When we hold onto grudges, resentments, and anger towards others, it can lead to feelings of unhappiness and discontentment in our lives.

If you're unable to forgive people, you'll experience an emotional burden that will cause you to dwell on negative experiences from the past.

This could lead to bitterness and anger, which will negatively influence your overall emotional well-being.

Unforgiveness could also cause you not to trust people and, as a result, you might struggle to form meaningful relationships.

This could make you feel isolated and unhappy.

When you're able to forgive people and let go of grudges and resentments, you're more likely to experience joy and contentment.

The Benefits of Forgiveness

While unforgiveness can have negative effects on your health, there are many benefits to forgiving someone.

One of the most important things you will do is reduce your stress level, as holding onto resentment and grudges will only increase it. If you can forgive and let go of anger, you'll be a much calmer person.

When you release those feelings, you'll be a better communicator who can healthily resolve conflicts.

Forgiveness will help you to be happier, and you're much more likely to experience peace, joy, and contentment. It will have a positive effect on your mental health and will reduce your symptoms of anxiety and depression. Plus, and will help you to improve your self-confidence and self-esteem.

Empathy and Forgiveness

Empathy and the ability to forgive greatly impact our relationships with others.

Forgiveness involves releasing negative emotions and choosing to move forward, without seeking revenge or holding a grudge.

Having empathy for someone who has wronged us can make it easier to forgive them, as we can understand their motivations and perspectives. Similarly, forgiving someone can help us cultivate empathy, as we can better understand their struggles and shortcomings.

How Does Empathy Help Us Forgive?

Empathy can lead to forgiveness by allowing us to understand the perspective of the person who has wronged us. When we can see things from their point of view, we may gain a better understanding of why they acted the way they did, which can make it easier to forgive them.

For example, if someone makes a hurtful comment towards us, it can be easy to feel angry or resentful towards them. However, if we take a moment to consider their situation and motivations, we may realize that they were under a lot of stress or dealing with personal struggles that caused them to act out. By putting ourselves in their shoes, we may feel more compassion toward them and be more willing to pardon them.

Empathy can also help us to see the humanity in others, even when they have hurt us. When we can recognize that everyone makes mistakes and has flaws, it can be easier to extend forgiveness and move on from the situation.

When we practice compassion toward others, we're more likely to engage in open and honest communication with the person who has wronged us. This can help to clarify misunderstandings, address underlying issues, and find a path toward reconciliation.

The Importance of Forgiving the Past

Some of us find it easy to hold onto grudges, for a variety of reasons.

We hold on to negative emotions towards someone who has done something to wrong us because we feel this will keep us from being harmed by the same person again. After all, we know better now than to trust them, and we may even develop feelings of distrust toward other people who remind us of this person.

We could also feel that carrying a grudge gives us power over those who have harmed us. In a sense, we're "punishing" them by harboring continued negative feelings towards them. Sadly, holding onto a grudge could become part of *your* identity. You may start seeing yourself as a "victim," and then feel you have to hold on to anger and resentment to maintain that identity.

It could also become a habit to hold onto a grudge, especially if we have done it for a long time. It can be difficult to break the cycle of negative emotions and move toward forgiveness and healing.

It could be difficult to forgive someone because we don't understand their perspectives and emotions. Without this realization, it may be hard to let go of bitterness and move toward peace.

Forgive Yourself for a Happier Life

Forgiving yourself will help you create a happier life for yourself.

When we hold onto guilt and shame over past mistakes, it can weigh us down and make it difficult to move forward. Forgiving yourself can help you release the past, and focus on the present and future.

Forgiving yourself can also improve your self-esteem. When you can let go of self-blame and accept yourself for who you are, you may feel more confident and self-assured.

When you liberate yourself, you may also find that you are better able to form positive relationships with others. This is because you are no longer burdened by negative self-talk or self-doubt, which can create barriers to connection and intimacy.

Forgiving yourself can also help you to cultivate compassion toward yourself and others. When you can accept your imperfections, you may be more forgiving of yourself, which can help you to become more resilient. When you can bounce back from mistakes and setbacks without getting bogged down in self-blame and negative emotions, you may be better equipped to handle challenges and adversity.

Steps You Can Take to Forgive Yourself

It can be a challenge to forgive yourself, but there are things you can do to make it easier for yourself and those around you.

The first step in forgiving yourself is to acknowledge the negative emotions that you're experiencing. This might include guilt, shame, or self-blame. Be honest with yourself about what you're feeling, and allow yourself to experience those emotions.

Treat yourself with kindness, understanding, and acceptance. Instead of berating yourself for past mistakes, try to approach yourself with compassion and empathy. Remind yourself that everyone makes mistakes and that you are worthy of forgiveness and love.

While it's important to be compassionate towards yourself, it's also important to take responsibility for your actions. You need to acknowledge how you may have hurt others or yourself, and commit to making amends or changes where possible.

Negative self-talk can make it difficult to forgive yourself. Try to reframe your thoughts in a more positive light. For example, when something goes wrong, don't think you'll never be able to achieve something; instead, reaffirm that you'll learn from your mistakes and do better next time.

Forgiving Past Hurts and Trauma

It's not easy, and it may not be possible, for some people to forgive those who have traumatized them in the past.

Acknowledge the trauma the abuser has caused you, and the impact their actions have had on you. You need to feel and express the emotions that arise when you think about the trauma.

During the healing process, you need to take especially good care of yourself. This could involve taking part in activities you enjoy and surrounding yourself with supportive people.

Set boundaries that will protect you from experiencing more harm. This could involve limiting or cutting off contact with the person who has traumatized you. You also need to set clear expectations of how you want to be treated.

Try to see the actions from the perpetrator's point of view. This doesn't mean you should condone their actions, but it could help to see the situation from a different viewpoint.

Try to be empathetic, if possible, and feel compassion for the other person's experiences and emotions. This could also help you to let go of feelings of resentment and anger.

Try to accept what has happened, and let go of the need for revenge and retribution. This could be difficult, but can also help you heal.

When You Should Forgive, but Keep Your Distance

While forgiveness can be a powerful tool for healing and moving on from difficult situations, there may be times when you can forgive someone, but then keep your distance from them as much as possible, or cut them from your life altogether.

If you forgive someone who is still engaging in harmful behavior, you may just be putting yourself or anyone close to you at risk. For example, an abuser who becomes violent may put the physical health, or even the lives, of you and your children at risk. In this case, you should prioritize your well-being and that of your family. You can still forgive the person, but maintain your distance for the sake of everyone's safety.

It may also take you some time to get to the point where you're able to forgive someone who harmed you. It's a personal process that everyone should manage at their own pace. You need to give yourself enough time and room in which to heal.

Forgiving in Advance

Forgiving in advance means letting go of any potential anger or resentment towards someone before they have even done something that might upset you. It involves choosing to trust and believe in someone's good intentions, and not holding grudges or negative feelings toward them based on past experiences or assumptions.

While forgiving ahead of time can be a positive mindset to have, it is important to balance it with healthy boundaries and communication. Forgiving in advance does not mean accepting harmful or abusive behavior, and it is still important to communicate your needs and concerns to the person you are interacting with.

Forgiving in advance can be a powerful tool for promoting positivity and reducing stress and conflict in relationships.

Anticipatory Forgiveness

You're practicing anticipatory forgiveness when you let go of negative feelings and resentment towards someone who hasn't yet acknowledged their wrongdoing or hasn't yet apologized.

It's a conscious decision to forgive someone before they asked you for forgiveness or tried to make any amends.

Anticipatory forgiveness can be helpful in situations where it may be difficult, or even impossible, to receive an apology, or closure, from the other person—such as when the person has passed away or you no longer have contact with the person. It can also be useful when holding onto anger and resentment could cause harm to your mental health.

It's vital to note, however, that this type of forgiveness doesn't mean excusing or condoning the other person's behavior. You still need to address the harm that has been caused and set boundaries to prevent it from happening again in the future.

There could be various situations where you may need to practice anticipatory forgiveness:

> When you know you will be interacting with someone who has previously hurt you or caused you pain, and you want to proactively let go of any negative feelings towards them. This is especially useful in a work situation, as working together can become a nightmare if coworkers hold resentments and unresolved situations get in the way of their productivity.

> When you have experienced a significant loss, such as the death of a loved one or the end of a relationship, and you want to forgive the person who caused you pain even if they are no longer in your life. You want to move on with your life, and it's no longer possible to speak to the person, so this is the best option.

> When you want to repair or improve a relationship, the other person may not be willing or able to apologize or make amends for their past actions. You could anticipate that similar situations can occur in the future, and you decide you need to let it go because you understand where the person is coming from. For example, they could have unresolved situations they need to work on.

> When you want to practice compassion and empathy towards others, even if they have not yet shown remorse or acknowledged their wrongdoings. For instance, if you understand the background and why someone is acting negatively. They could come from a dysfunctional home, or some other situation may have altered the way they react, and you might decide it's not worth it to hold their behavior against them.

Oprah Winfrey's Story—Self-forgiveness

Talented talk show host Oprah Winfrey has learned to forgive herself for many things through the years. She has openly talked about her struggles with weight, self-esteem, and other personal issues; furthermore, she has discussed the importance of self-forgiveness in overcoming these challenges.

Winfrey has had a complicated life and difficult childhood, but resilience has helped her to overcome the obstacles she had to face.

In her book *What I Know for Sure*, Oprah writes about how she used to feel guilty and ashamed about her bad decisions and past mistakes. She eventually realized that to achieve her goals and lead a happier life in general, she would need to learn to forgive herself.

Oprah has also spoken about her experience with sexual abuse and how she was able to forgive her abuser, which ultimately helped her to heal and move on from her traumatic childhood.

Through her journey, Oprah has become an advocate for self-forgiveness and has inspired many people to let go of their past mistakes and embrace a more positive and empowering future.

Key Takeaways

- ➤ When you hold onto grudges, resentments, and anger, it can lead to feelings of unhappiness and discontentment.
- ➤ Unforgiveness could make it difficult for you to form meaningful relationships.
- ➤ Forgiveness has a positive influence on our mental health and also helps us improve our self-esteem.
- ➤ Having empathy for someone who has wronged us can make it easier for us to forgive them since we're capable of understanding their motivations and perspectives.
- ➤ Sometimes we think that holding onto grudges will prevent us from being hurt again.
- ➤ We could even feel that holding onto negative feelings toward someone who has hurt us gives us power over them.
- ➤ Holding onto a grudge could become part of your identity. You could start seeing yourself as a "victim," and feel you have to hold onto anger and resentment to maintain that identity.
- ➤ Negative self-talk could make it difficult to forgive yourself. Reframe your thoughts in a more positive light.
- ➤ In some instances, it might not be a good idea to forgive those who have done you harm—for example, if this person is still engaging in harmful behavior that could put you and your family at risk.
- ➤ Anticipatory forgiveness means letting go of potential anger or resentment toward someone even before they've acknowledged wrongdoing or apologized to you.

Worksheet: Forgiveness and Self-Forgiveness

Instructions

This worksheet aims to help you incorporate forgiveness and self-forgiveness in your life. Write the answers to the questions below in your journal.

Part 1: Forgiveness

- Identify the person or situation that you need to forgive.
- Write down what specifically happened that caused you pain or hurt.
- Acknowledge your feelings towards the situation or person, such as anger, sadness, or resentment.
- Try to understand the other person's perspective and the reasons behind their actions. Write down any insights or realizations you have.
- Write a letter to the person or situation, expressing your forgiveness and letting go of any negative feelings you have been holding onto. You don't have to send the letter, but writing down your feelings can help you with the process of forgiveness.

Part 2: Self-Forgiveness

- Identify a situation where you feel like you need to forgive yourself.
- Write down what specifically happened and how it made you feel.

- ➢ Acknowledge any mistakes or wrongdoings you may have committed.
- ➢ Consider what you learned from the situation, and how you can grow from it.
- ➢ Write a letter to yourself expressing your forgiveness and compassion towards yourself. Remind yourself that you are only human and that you deserve forgiveness as much as anyone else.

Part 3: Reflection

- ➢ Think about the process of forgiveness and self-forgiveness. How did you feel when you let go of negative feelings and practiced forgiveness?
- ➢ Write down any insights or realizations you had during the forgiveness process.
- ➢ Consider other ways you can promote forgiveness and compassion in your life, such as practicing empathy towards others or setting healthy boundaries.

CHAPTER 6:
DECLUTTERING FOR A HAPPY AND STRESS-FREE LIFE

Decluttering is important for your mental health and can help you lead a calmer life.

Doing it regularly can help you reduce your stress level. A cluttered environment can be overwhelming, and getting rid of items that you don't use anymore can create a more peaceful space that promotes relaxation and peace of mind.

Clutter can also negatively impact your productivity, as it makes it difficult to focus on tasks and complete them efficiently. Decluttering promotes productivity. Your home will also be safer once it has been decluttered, as messy spaces increase the risk of accidents and injuries. Removing objects from an overcrowded space creates a secure environment, through clear and unobstructed spaces.

If your living area is so cluttered that you can't find things, decluttering will also save you money and time spent searching for them. Sometimes, we end up spending money on things we already have, simply because we can't find them.

Living in a cluttered environment could potentially harm your mental health, and lead to feelings of anxiety, depression, and overwhelm. Creating more space can make your environment more positive and uplifting.

What Is Mind Decluttering?

You know how to straighten up your house or other tangible items or areas, but what about your inner thoughts? Mind decluttering can also make you more focused, productive, and calmer.

Here are some simple tips to help you declutter your mind:

- ➤ Write things down. You need to get things out of your mind and onto paper, which will help you free up some mental space and help you gain clarity. You could write your thoughts in a journal, make lists, or use a task manager to organize your thoughts.
- ➤ Consider what is most important to you and prioritize your tasks accordingly. This can help you focus and prevents you from becoming bogged down by less important things.
- ➤ Practice meditation and mindfulness to clear your mind, help you focus, and be present in the moment. It could also help you develop greater awareness of your thoughts and emotions, which can help you identify and address the origins of your mental clutter.
- ➤ Reduce distractions like social media, email notifications, and other unnecessary rings and pings from technology devices. You'll avoid a great deal of mental clutter by limiting or taking a break from such interruptions.

- Do your best to let go of the pursuit to be perfect. Perfectionism can cause a lot of mental clutter, as you get bogged down by the idea of doing things flawlessly. Focus on the process, rather than achieving a perfect end product. Let go of unimportant things.
- Take breaks, even if they're short ones, throughout the day to give your brain a break. This will help you not to become overwhelmed or burnt out and permits you to reset and recharge.
- Make sure you get enough sleep, as sleep is vital for mental clarity and focus. Rest and take care of yourself, so that you can always perform at your best.

How Decluttering Impacts Happiness and Success

Decluttering your physical space can positively impact your emotional well-being. A cluttered environment can seem chaotic and could make us feel overwhelmed, thus contributing to increased stress levels. By decluttering your space, you can create a happier and more peaceful environment.

Clearing space can also make you more productive, and help you get tasks done faster. It could be difficult to focus on tasks when you're surrounded by mess and things you don't need. You'll often find that you'll have greater mental clarity and that your entire thinking process flows better when you're not surrounded by all kinds of objects that just take up useful space.

Freeing up space can also help you think more creatively and improve your mood. There's nothing worse than wanting to do something creative, but not having the space to do so.

It can be financially rewarding to declutter your home, as you could supplement your income by selling unwanted items. This could also help you make a conscious decision to buy what you really need in the future. After all, there's no point in filling up your home with new junk after you've just managed to create some useful open space!

Decluttering and Freedom From Stress

Decluttering could even help prevent burnout. We experience burnout —or emotional, physical, and mental exhaustion—when we have chronic stress in our work or personal lives.

Burnout causes us to feel overwhelmed, exhausted, cynical, and detached from our responsibilities and relationships. People who are burned out may often feel drained, and struggle to keep on performing at their best.

Burnout could be the result of work-related stress, long hours, lack of autonomy, and feeling disconnected from one's work or coworkers. We also feel burned out in our personal relationships, when we feel emotionally drained from constantly giving without receiving support in return.

It's important to recognize the signs of burnout, and then take steps to manage and prevent it.

Decluttering can also be a helpful tool in preventing burnout because reducing clutter can reduce stress and create a more calming environment. After decluttering, what about creating a dedicated space for relaxation and self-care? Add plants, soothing music, scented candles, comfortable seating, relaxing reading material, or a yoga mat. It's easier to prioritize your self-care if you have your own dedicated space.

When your environment is too cluttered, becomes difficult to separate your work and personal life. By cleaning up and creating functional areas, you can promote a healthy work-life balance which will help you to prevent burnout.

Hoarding Disorder and Decluttering

Hoarding disorder is a mental health disorder where the sufferers find it difficult, and nearly impossible, to part with their possessions, regardless of their value. These people usually have extremely cluttered living spaces, which can affect their quality of life and also make it difficult for them to function daily.

Decluttering might cause tremendous anxiety and distress for people who suffer from hoarding disorder. However, it's possible to manage the symptoms with support and guidance.

If you feel decluttering could benefit you, even if you suffer from this disorder, you could consider the following:

- Get professional help from a therapist who has experience in managing this disorder. They can help you work on strategies that will make it easier for you to manage your hoarding behavior.
- You may find you need a plan, or learn strategies, to manage the decluttering process. For instance, you could sort your possessions into categories, or use a timer to limit how much time you spend on a certain task. You could also create a plan that breaks down the tasks into smaller steps. This could help you reduce feelings of anxiety.
- Make sure you start your decluttering with items that are less important to you and have less emotional value. First, practice your decision-making skills on these items, such as clothing or kitchen items as this process can help you build confidence. Later, you can move on to more sentimental items like photos or books.

> You could also consider an approach of harm reduction if you suffer from this disorder. For example, rather than attempting to eliminate clutter completely, set a goal for yourself to create a safe and functional living space. Set a limit on the amount of clutter in your home, or set the target of decluttering one room at a time.

How to Do a Thorough Mind Declutter

Mindfulness can be a powerful tool to reduce mental clutter. For this purpose, you should focus on the present, observe your thoughts without judging them, and let them pass.

Mental and physical clutter can be equally overwhelming. Our minds are constantly processing information and—when they become overloaded—we can experience stress, anxiety, and mental fatigue.

So, how can mindfulness help us declutter our minds?

Mindfulness helps us become more aware of our thoughts, feelings, and sensations. This awareness can help us identify the sources of mental clutter and work to address them.

It also helps us observe our thoughts without judgment. This can help us let go of negative self-talk, and reduce the mental clutter that comes from dwelling on our shortcomings or mistakes. Mindfulness can also help us not to clutter our minds with worries about what will happen in the future, or what happened in the past.

Mindfulness involves accepting our thoughts and feelings as they are, without trying to change them. This can help reduce the mental clutter that comes from trying to suppress, or ignore, our thoughts and feelings. It also helps us to take notice of our thought patterns.

Mindfulness techniques, such as deep breathing or progressive muscle relaxation, can help reduce stress and promote relaxation—leading to a clearer and more focused mind.

How to Declutter Your Mind

Decluttering your mind may sound daunting, but there are plenty of easy ways that you can go about doing this:

- Write down your thoughts to help you clear your mind. If you write everything down, it will make it easier to prioritize if you can see it on paper.
- Create to-do lists to organize your tasks. This is especially useful when it comes to reducing the mental burden of having to remember everything.
- Take regular breaks from technology and social media, to help your mind rest and refocus.
- Spend time outside in nature to help you clear your mind and take a much-needed break from your work day.
- Meditation can help you to let go of negative emotions and thoughts, which will help you be more focused. Deep breathing could also help you calm your mind.
- Make a list of things for which you are grateful. This could help you get rid of some of the negative thoughts in your mind and shift the focus to what is positive.
- Make your self-talk as positive as possible. Negative self-talk can also clutter your mind.
- Make sure you practice enough self-care to stay healthy. Eat enough, sleep enough, and make sure you get regular exercise.

> Say *no* to commitments or invitations that don't align with your priorities and values, as this can help you free up mental space. Time is limited, and most people don't have the time to commit to activities that don't interest them.
> Creative activities like writing, painting, or drawing can also help you clear your mind and express your thoughts and feelings.

How to Do a Thorough Relationship Declutter

Managing your relationships is about creating space for positive, healthy connections. It may be difficult at first, but the result will be worth it.

You can usually start to pick up on the signs when it's time to declutter your relationships. If you find that you feel drained and exhausted after spending time with certain people in your life, it may be a sign that it's time to let them go. If a relationship is not positively serving you, there is no point in continuing it.

If you feel undervalued and unsupported in a relationship, like you just keep on giving and receiving nothing in return, it might be time to reconsider this relationship.

If your needs and desires aren't respected or heard, is it worth your while to continue it?

If you dread spending time with certain people and make excuses not to see them, the relationship is not healthy or worth continuing.

The same goes for people who make you feel like you're walking on eggshells. If you have to tiptoe around people to avoid conflict, the relationship is not built on mutual respect and trust.

If a relationship is holding you back from growing and evolving, it's also time to re-evaluate it. If it's holding you back from pursuing your dreams and goals, it needs to go.

It's vital to always prioritize your *own* mental and emotional well-being in any relationship. If a relationship isn't healthy, it's time to let it go.

Practical Steps to Declutter Your Relationships

The first thing you need to do, when you're going to manage your relationships, is to assess them and identify the toxic ones. Look at which relationships bring you joy, and which ones just drain your energy. End or phase out the bad relationships and focus on the supportive, healthy ones.

When you have identified relationships that aren't going well, set boundaries with the people involved. This could involve limiting your time with them or avoiding certain topics of conversation. If they're extremely toxic, it might be a good idea to avoid seeing them altogether.

If a relationship is causing you stress or discomfort, have an honest conversation with the people involved and tell them how you're feeling.

They could be unaware of how their behavior is impacting you. Start relationships with positive people. Surround yourself with people who are supportive and emotionally uplifting. Spending time with people who share your values and interests can help you feel more fulfilled and energized.

Decluttering with Marie Kondo

Marie Kondo is a celebrity who believes in the importance of decluttering. She is an organizing consultant from Japan who wrote the best-selling book *The Life-Changing Magic of Tidying Up*. She is also the host of the Netflix series *Tidying Up with Marie Kondo*.

DECLUTTERING FOR A HAPPY AND STRESS-FREE LIFE

Kondo believes that you should only keep the things that bring you joy in life. Her method involves sorting through all of one's possessions and discarding those that no longer serve a purpose or "spark joy". She also emphasizes that it's important to organize items in a way that makes them easy to find.

Kondo's approach has gained a lot of popularity, and she has also inspired a wider conversation about minimalism and the benefits of living with less.

Kondo's philosophy is known as the KonMari method and involves the following steps:

- Visualize the kind of lifestyle you want to have and the type of environment you want to live in.
- Before you begin decluttering, commit to tidying up and creating a more organized space.
- Before you organize things, you should first discard some of them. Go through all your possessions and decide what you want to keep and what you want to let go of.
- Her most famous principle is that you should only keep those things that bring you joy. Let go of items that no longer serve a purpose or bring you happiness.
- Sort your items by category, rather than by location. This means gathering all items of a certain type (such as clothing or books) in one place and sorting through them all at once.
- Follow a specific order for sorting your things. For example, begin with clothes, then move on to books, papers, and other items.

- Organize your remaining items by category, in a way that makes them easy to find.

Key Takeaways

- Create a column for the relationships in your life including family, friends, coworkers, and acquaintances.
- Using a scale of 1–10, rate each relationship based on how positive and fulfilling it is for you.
- Look at the relationships with low ratings. Which relationships bring you down, cause stress, or leave you feeling drained or exhausted?
- For each negative relationship, think about what boundaries you need to set to protect yourself. This could include limiting your time with that person, avoiding certain topics of conversation, or being more assertive about your needs and boundaries. Write down the boundaries you have decided to set next to each person's name.
- If a relationship is consistently negative, toxic, or abusive—it may be time to let it go. Write down what steps you need to take to let go of that relationship such as setting clear boundaries, gradually reducing contact, or seeking support from a therapist or counselor. Indicate these steps next to each person's name.
- Make a list of the positive relationships. Think about how you can nurture those relationships and spend more time with those people. Write the ideas down next to each person's name.

Activity—Declutter Your Relationships

Pay close attention when you read the instructions below. You can complete the activities in writing in your journal, or on one of your electronic devices.

- ➤ Create a column for the relationships in your life including family, friends, coworkers, and acquaintances.
- ➤ Using a scale of 1–10, rate each relationship based on how positive and fulfilling it is for you.
- ➤ Look at the relationships with low ratings. Which relationships bring you down, cause stress, or leave you feeling drained or exhausted?
- ➤ For each negative relationship, think about what boundaries you need to set to protect yourself. This could include limiting your time with that person, avoiding certain topics of conversation, or being more assertive about your needs and boundaries. Write down the boundaries you have decided to set next to each person's name.
- ➤ If a relationship is consistently negative, toxic, or abusive—it may be time to let it go. Write down what steps you need to take to let go of that relationship such as setting clear boundaries, gradually reducing contact, or seeking support from a therapist or counselor. Indicate these steps next to each person's name.
- ➤ Make a list of the positive relationships. Think about how you can nurture those relationships and spend more time with those people. Write the ideas down next to each person's name.

CHAPTER 7:
STOP TOXIC EMOTIONS AND BUILD POSITIVITY

Emotions are important because they can determine how you think and behave. Emotions are what make us human, and they play an important role in our ability to navigate the world around us and interact with others.

Why Emotions Are Useful

Emotions serve several important functions in our lives. They allow us to communicate our needs, desires, and feelings to others. For example, if we feel happy, we may express this by smiling or laughing; and, if we feel sad, we may cry or withdraw.

Emotions help us make decisions by providing us with information about what we value and what is important to us. Thus, if we feel fear, it may be a signal that we need to avoid a certain situation or take precautions to protect ourselves.

They can also help us determine if a situation is safe or dangerous. Therefore, if we feel anxious, we may decide to avoid a certain situation.

Emotions help us empathize with others, which makes it easier to form healthy relationships. For example, feeling happy when someone else is happy can help us feel closer to them and build stronger relationships.

Where Do Our Emotions Come From?

To understand our emotions, we also need to know more about where they come from.

Our emotions originate as a result of complicated interactions between different parts of our brains and are also the result of external stimuli and past experiences.

From a physiological perspective, the amygdala is the small structure in our brains that is responsible for processing emotions, especially ones like fear and aggression. The prefrontal cortex, which also accounts for higher-level thinking, is involved with the regulation of decision-making.

Hormones, such as adrenaline and cortisol, additionally play a role in triggering emotional responses and preparing the body for action.

Our memories of past experiences can determine how we respond to new situations, especially if we have had traumatic or highly emotional experiences in the past. People who have experienced childhood trauma, for instance, can be triggered by certain events as adults.

Cultural and social norms can influence how we express and interpret emotions, as well as which emotions are considered appropriate in different contexts.

For example, we may have been taught as children that it's unacceptable to express our anger, or that we're not supposed to cry, in certain situations.

The Role of Childhood Trauma

Negative experiences during childhood can affect our ability to develop self-love. Childhood caretakers may have led us to believe negative things about ourselves, especially if they were overly critical.

Childhood experiences can unfortunately cause people to develop feelings of shame and worthlessness which last into adult life. This can make it especially difficult for people to develop a sense of self-worth.

Neglect and abandonment can send a message to children that there is something wrong with them, and that they are not worthy of someone's time, love, and attention.

In adulthood, many people who have been treated like this create false personalities to distance themselves from their memories of childhood trauma.

People live behind this mask to hide their feelings and needs from others. It also helps them to conform to social expectations, especially of their family and friends.

This people-pleasing behavior often leads to inauthentic lifestyles. This could make it difficult for people to form genuine relationships; thus, they struggle to connect to others on a deeper level, which often leads to social isolation and further emotional distress.

Therapy will probably be needed to overcome post-traumatic stress (PTSD)—which is often associated with trauma—and also to develop an authentic sense of self and to develop self-love. This can be a long process, but it's ultimately worthwhile for trauma survivors to do the work, to build a better life for themselves.

Getting in Touch with Your Emotions

It is especially difficult to get in touch with your emotions if you're used to suppressing them. However, there are ways you can become more aware of your emotions and express them in healthy ways.

Mindfulness is a powerful tool for increasing emotional awareness. By focusing on the present moment, without judgment, you can become more attuned to your emotional experiences.

Writing down your thoughts and feelings in a journal can help you process and understand your emotions. Take time each day to write about your experiences and think about how you feel. If you don't have time to do it daily, try to do so at least weekly.

Your body can also provide important clues about your emotional state. Pay attention to physical sensations, such as muscle tension or stomach discomfort, as these may be signals of underlying stress or fear.

Creative activities—such as art, music, or dance—can help you tap into your emotions and express them nonverbally. These forms of expression can be especially useful if you're struggling to say in words *exactly* what you feel.

You might not, yet, be entirely sure what you're feeling; therefore, partaking in creative activities might help you uncover more feelings.

Remember that becoming more in touch with your emotions is a process, and it may take time and practice to develop greater emotional awareness.

You need to be patient with yourself and talk to a therapist if you think you need to do so. It's also a good idea to read more about developing emotional intelligence.

When You Don't Accept Your Emotions

If you suppress your emotions, you may (unfortunately) experience negative consequences. These could include the following:

> - Emotional distress in the form of anxiety and depression. This could be a complicated situation, as many people learn in childhood that it's unacceptable to express certain emotions.
> - Unpleasant physical symptoms such as headaches, fatigue, and muscle tension. Suppressing your emotions could place a lot of stress on your body.
> - Difficulty relating to others and understanding their emotional experiences, leading to relationship problems.
> - The development of unhealthy coping mechanisms such as substance abuse or self-harm.
> - Poor decision-making, as you may be ignoring important information about your needs and desires.

It's important to acknowledge and accept your emotions, as you can then learn to regulate them healthily and improve your overall well-being.

How to Share Your Emotions

Sharing your emotions can be a vulnerable and challenging experience, but it can also be an important part of building healthy relationships and coping with difficult situations. These tips can help you share your emotions effectively:

> - Choose the right time and place where you feel comfortable and safe to share your emotions. Ensure that you have privacy and enough time to have a meaningful conversation.

STOP TOXIC EMOTIONS AND BUILD POSITIVITY

- Use "I" statements to express how you feel, rather than blaming or accusing the other person. For example, say, "It makes me sad when you don't listen" instead of "You never listen to me."
- Try to be as specific as possible. Use examples and provide context to help the other person understand how you are feeling. Express yourself carefully because you don't want the other person to feel as if you're blaming them for your negative emotions.
- Listen to the other person's perspective when you share your sentiments. Show empathy and try to understand their point of view. While you need to express your perspective, there needs to be a balance, and you always need to try to understand other people's viewpoints.
- Be open to feedback and suggestions from the other person, but remember that you have the right to set boundaries and communicate your needs.
- When the other person is sharing their thoughts and feelings, practice active listening by paying attention, asking questions, and reflecting back on what you hear.

Meaning and Examples of Toxic Emotions

Toxic emotions are bad for your mental and physical well-being. They could be anything from mild feelings of frustration or disappointment—to intense emotions like anger, resentment, or hatred. The following are examples of toxic emotions:

- Anger can be a positive emotion in certain circumstances but when it is not expressed or managed healthily, it can lead to destructive behavior and can be harmful to yourself and others.

- Resentment is a feeling of bitterness or anger that arises from past experiences or perceived injustices. Holding onto it can lead to negative thoughts and behaviors that can harm relationships.
- Guilt is a feeling of remorse or regret for past actions or behaviors. Excessive guilt or self-blame can lead to low self-esteem.
- Jealousy is a feeling of envy or resentment towards others who have something that you want. Excessive jealousy can damage your relationships.
- Shame is a feeling of deep embarrassment or humiliation that arises from feelings of inadequacy or failure. This could also lead to low self-esteem.

It's important to recognize these toxic emotions and learn how to manage them healthily.

Toxic Emotions Can Make You Sick

Toxic emotions can make you sick, so if you're struggling emotionally, look out for the following physical symptoms:

- Prolonged stress and negative emotions, like anxiety and depression, can weaken your immune system; hence, you can find that you get sick more often. You might even be more susceptible to infections that take a longer time to heal.
- Toxic emotions like anger, resentment, and frustration have been linked to an increased risk of chronic diseases like heart disease, diabetes, and cancer. A "cancer personality" has even been identified, which consists mainly of people who suppress their emotions.

- Toxic emotions can make it difficult to sleep, which can lead to chronic insomnia and sleep disorders. This is especially true if you're prone to rumination—which means that negative thoughts will repeat in your head over and over again.
- Negative emotions, like anger and anxiety, can cause a temporary increase in blood pressure, which can have long-term effects on your heart health.
- Toxic emotions can also impact your digestive system, causing symptoms like nausea, bloating, and diarrhea.
- Prolonged toxic emotions can lead to mental health problems like depression, anxiety, and post-traumatic stress disorder (PTSD).

Toxic emotions should be managed healthily. This means you may need to see a therapist or practice stress-reducing activities like meditation, exercise, or spending time in nature.

How Toxic Emotions Impact Happiness

Toxic emotions can certainly harm our overall sense of well-being and happiness. When we experience sensations like anger, jealousy, resentment, and bitterness—they can consume our thoughts and cause us to feel unhappy, stressed, or anxious. These feelings can interfere with our ability to enjoy life and maintain healthy relationships.

It's important to acknowledge and address our toxic emotions, rather than suppressing or ignoring them, as this can lead to further emotional distress. One way to do this is by practicing mindfulness and self-awareness, which involves recognizing our emotions and learning to observe them, without judgment. From there, we can work on developing coping strategies—such as talking to a trusted friend or therapist, engaging in physical activity, or practicing relaxation techniques.

You need to acknowledge your toxic emotions and deal with them; otherwise, they will just hold you captive, and prevent you from completing your journey to love yourself.

Positive Emotions Lead to Greater Happiness

Positive emotions can lead to greater resilience, which can help us bounce back from bad times faster and move on with our lives.

When we experience emotions like joy, gratitude, and hope, they can help us build emotional resources that we can draw upon during challenging times. For instance, if we have a strong sense of hope, we will be more likely to persevere through difficult circumstances and believe that things will ultimately get better.

Additionally, positive emotions can help us develop a sense of social support, which is another important factor in resilience. When we experience positive emotions in the context of our relationships with others, it can strengthen those relationships and help us feel more connected to others. This sense of connection and support can help us better cope with adversity and build our resilience.

Positive emotions are also strongly associated with greater life satisfaction. When we experience pleasant vibes—such as joy, contentment, and gratitude—we usually have a more positive outlook on life.

By experiencing positive emotions more frequently, we can cultivate an optimistic mindset that will help us to create a buffer against the negative effects of stress and adversity we experience daily.

Why You Must Deal With Toxic Emotions

It's possible to deal with toxic emotions healthily, but many people tend to develop unhealthy coping mechanisms—such as substance abuse, self-harm, overeating, or undereating—which can evolve into full-blown eating disorders. Others turn to overwork as a way to avoid their emotions, but this could lead to burnout and further emotional distress, driving a wedge between them and their loved ones.

Some people avoid their emotions altogether, but this can cause even worse distress over a longer period when the root causes of negative emotions are never addressed. Bottled-up emotions can become mental health disorders or lead to undesirable behavior, such as lashing out at others.

Managing Your Negative Emotions

It's essential to manage your negative emotions, for the sake of your mental, physical, and relational health.

Negative emotions can also impact professional success by impacting your productivity, relationships with coworkers, and overall job satisfaction. You'll perform better at work and have more success in achieving your career goals if you manage your emotions productively.

You'll also feel more in control of your emotions and happiness if you learn to identify and manage your toxic emotions. For example, if you feel the need to argue with someone because you're angry or jealous about something they said, first try to name the specific emotion, and then decide why it's making you feel this way. Consider if an argument would be worth it, and whether it's possible to reframe the scenario more positively. Could you communicate your feelings to the other person differently?

Developing healthy coping strategies, and seeking support when needed, can help us effectively manage negative emotions and promote emotional well-being.

Coping with Toxic Emotions—Michelle Obama's Story

Michelle Obama had to learn to cope with toxic emotions while she was in the public eye as former U.S. President Barack Obama's wife. In her memoir *Becoming*, she writes about her struggles with imposter syndrome, anxiety, and depression, and how she has learned to manage these emotions.

Michelle has talked openly about seeking therapy to help her cope with the stress and pressure of her public role as First Lady. She has also emphasized the importance of self-care and taking time for herself, even at times when her schedule was very busy and demanding.

Through her journey, Michelle Obama has become an advocate for mental health and wellness and has encouraged others to seek help and support when dealing with difficult emotions. She has shown that it is possible to overcome toxic emotions and live a fulfilling and meaningful life.

Key Takeaways

- Emotions are important, as they influence our thoughts and behavior.
- Emotions help us to communicate our needs, desires, and feelings to others.
- Our feelings can help us to empathize with others, which makes it easier to form meaningful relationships.

STOP TOXIC EMOTIONS AND BUILD POSITIVITY

- Our emotions are the result of interactions among the different parts of our brains, external stimuli, and past experiences.
- There are different ways in which you can get in touch with your emotions. One is to write down your thoughts and feelings.
- If you suppress your emotions, you may experience negative consequences. Some of the unpleasant physical symptoms can include headaches, fatigue, and muscle tension.
- It's important to choose a time and place that makes you feel safe enough to share your emotions.
- Toxic emotions can be bad for your overall well-being. These could be anything from mild feelings of frustration to intense emotions of anger and hatred.
- Toxic emotions can even make you sick and cause all kinds of health problems.
- Positive feelings can help us develop greater resilience.

Activity: Get in Touch with Your Emotions

Instructions

- Find a quiet, comfortable place to sit where you won't be interrupted.
- Think about your week, or day, and identify a situation that triggered an emotional response in you.
- Write the situation down in your journal, and think about the emotions it made you feel. Use descriptive words and write your feelings down. It's very important to identify the specific emotions that you felt.

- Think about the emotions you experienced in more detail. Write down your thoughts and the beliefs that may have contributed to your emotion, as well as the physical sensations you experienced.
- Were the emotions you experienced helpful or unhelpful? Did they aid you in taking positive action, or were you unable to respond effectively?
- Write down what you've learned from this exercise. How can you manage your emotions more effectively in the future?

CHAPTER 8:
SELF-CARE, PEACE OF MIND, AND DAILY HAPPINESS

As we have seen so far, taking care of yourself is essential to maintaining your physical, emotional, and mental well-being. It is a crucial part of maintaining good health and preventing burnout, and shouldn't be considered selfish.

Self-care helps you recharge your batteries, manage stress, and maintain a positive outlook on life. When you take care of yourself, you are better equipped to take care of others and to be productive in your work and personal life. These things can't be stressed enough, which is why they're being repeated!

It's important to remember that self-care is not just about pampering yourself or indulging in activities you enjoy. It can also involve making healthy choices such as getting enough sleep, eating a balanced diet, exercising regularly, getting regular health checks with your dentist and doctor, and asking for help when you need it.

Neglecting self-care can lead to negative consequences such as decreased productivity, poor health, and increased stress levels. So, taking care of yourself is not only beneficial for you, but it also benefits those around you. Therefore, self-care is not selfish, but rather a responsible and necessary part of maintaining your well-being.

All-Around Guide to Self-Care And Happiness

Self-care advice may seem very similar in many instances, but there are different types of self-care you can practice.

> ➢ Physical self-care involves taking care of your body. This includes things like getting enough sleep, eating a healthy diet, exercising regularly, and taking care of any physical health concerns you may have by consulting your doctor or dentist early. Our physical health is one of the most precious things that we'll ever have in our lives, as it becomes difficult to do anything else if we're not physically healthy.
>
> ➢ Looking after your emotional and mental well-being is regarded as emotional self-care. This includes things like practicing mindfulness, seeking therapy or counseling if needed, and engaging in activities that help you manage stress and anxiety. It's so much easier to reach your goals in life if your emotional life is under control.
>
> ➢ Social self-care means nurturing your relationships with others. This includes spending time with friends and family, building new relationships, and setting boundaries to protect your mental

SELF-CARE, PEACE OF MIND, AND DAILY HAPPINESS

and emotional health in social situations. It could also involve letting go of toxic relationships.

- ➢ Spiritual self-care involves connecting with your spiritual or religious beliefs. This can include attending religious services, practicing meditation or yoga, or spending time in nature.

- ➢ Intellectual self-care refers to engaging in activities that stimulate your mind and challenge you intellectually. This can include reading, learning a new skill or hobby, or taking a class or workshop. It's vital to cultivate a lifelong learning mentality and keep discovering new skills and interests throughout your life.

- ➢ Professional self-care encompasses taking care of your career and work-related well-being. This can include setting boundaries between work and personal life, maintaining a good work-leisure balance, seeking support and resources from your coworkers or supervisors, and developing skills that you will need for your career.

- ➢ Environmental self-care entails creating a nurturing and supportive physical environment. This can include things like decluttering your living space, spending time in nature, or creating a relaxing and calming atmosphere in your home or workspace.

Self-care is about playing an active role in caring for your body, mind, and soul, and making intentional choices to support your physical, emotional, and mental health. It is essential to remember that you can't care for others if you don't care for yourself first.

Physical Self-Care

Here are some examples of physical self-care activities:

- ➢ Exercise is one of the best ways to maintain physical health and well-being. You can engage in a variety of activities—from cardio workouts to weight lifting, yoga, or Pilates. Pick one or more that you find enjoyable and are likely to continue with regularly.

- ➢ A healthy diet is essential for physical health and well-being. It includes eating a variety of nutrient-dense unprocessed foods such as fruits, vegetables, whole grains, lean proteins, and healthy fats. Also, allow yourself to have the occasional treat. An overly restrictive diet could be a sign of an eating disorder.

- ➢ Getting enough sleep is crucial for physical health and well-being. Most adults need at least seven hours of sleep each night to function at their best.

- ➢ Regular check-ups with your doctor or other healthcare providers can help identify any health concerns early and prevent potential problems.

- ➢ Drinking enough water is important for maintaining good physical fitness. The recommended daily intake is around eight glasses of water, consumed throughout the day.

- ➢ Self-massage can help relax tense muscles, reduce stress, and promote relaxation.

- ➢ Taking breaks and rest days will help your body to recover and recharge. It can also help prevent injuries and burnout.

SELF-CARE, PEACE OF MIND, AND DAILY HAPPINESS

Emotional Self-Care

Emotional self-care refers to activities that promote emotional well-being and help you manage stress, anxiety, and other negative emotions. The following are examples of emotional self-care activities:

- ➢ Practicing mindfulness and meditation can help you stay grounded and focused, reduce stress and anxiety, and improve overall emotional health.

- ➢ Writing your thoughts and emotions in a journal can help you process your emotions, and gain clarity on your thoughts and feelings. You'll often feel better if you can put some distance between yourself and toxic thoughts.

- ➢ Seeking therapy or counseling can be an effective way to address and manage emotional issues and mental health concerns.

- ➢ Taking part in activities that you enjoy—such as reading, painting, or gardening—can help reduce stress and promote emotional well-being.

- ➢ Setting healthy boundaries with others can help you maintain emotional balance and protect your mental health. You shouldn't feel the need to maintain a relationship that you feel is toxic to your well-being. It's good practice to evaluate your relationships regularly and determine if any of them are toxic to your overall health.

- ➢ Practicing self-compassion involves treating yourself with the same kindness as you would treat a close friend.

Social Self-Care

Social self-care entails becoming involved with activities that promote forming healthy relationships and connections with others. The following are examples of social self-care activities:

- ➢ Spending time with family and friends can help you feel connected and supported, reducing feelings of loneliness and isolation.

- ➢ Volunteering can be an excellent way to connect with others and give back to the community. Helping others will also distract you from your negative thoughts.

- ➢ Joining a social group or club can provide opportunities to connect with like-minded individuals who share your interests.

- ➢ Having meaningful conversations with others can help build deeper connections and promote emotional soundness.

- ➢ Practicing active listening involves fully engaging with others and showing genuine interest in what they have to say.

- ➢ Practicing forgiveness means letting go of grudges and resentments, and focusing on moving forward with positive relationships.

SELF-CARE, PEACE OF MIND, AND DAILY HAPPINESS

Spiritual Self-Care

Spiritual self-care refers to activities that promote a sense of connection to something greater than oneself and can help foster inner peace and a sense of purpose. It involves exploring and nurturing your spiritual beliefs and practices. Here are some examples of spiritual self-care activities:

- Meditation and prayer can help promote feelings of inner peace and spiritual connection.
- Attending religious or spiritual services can help foster a sense of community, and provide opportunities for reflection, service, and connection.
- Spending time in nature—such as hiking or gardening—can help you feel more connected to the world around you.
- Engaging in creative activities (e.g., writing, painting, or music) can help you with self-expression.
- Reading spiritual texts can inspire and guide you in exploring your spiritual beliefs.
- Practicing gratitude involves focusing on the positive aspects of life and being grateful for them.
- Reflecting on your values and beliefs can help you gain clarity on your spiritual path and what is most important to you.

Intellectual Self-Care

Intellectual self-care refers to activities that stimulate your mind and challenge you intellectually. This could be learning new skills, exploring new interests, and expanding your knowledge and understanding of the world in any way you can. Cultivate a lifelong learning mentality.

The following are examples of intellectual self-care activities:

- Reading is a great way to challenge your mind and expand your knowledge. You can read books, newspapers, or magazines on a variety of topics that interest you.
- It can be rewarding to learn different languages. It not only expands your intellectual capacity but also broadens your cultural horizons.
- Taking a course or class can help you learn new skills, improve your knowledge, and challenge yourself intellectually. You can take classes in a variety of subjects, from history and science to art and music. Many free courses are available online.
- Attending lectures or talks on a variety of topics can be an excellent way to learn and expand your knowledge. You can attend lectures at a local university or community center, or even watch or listen to online lectures or podcasts.
- Playing brain games like Sudoku, crosswords, logic puzzles, or chess can help improve cognitive function and stimulate the mind.
- Writing or journaling can help improve your cognitive and emotional well-being. It can also help you explore your thoughts and ideas in a creative and stimulating way.

SELF-CARE, PEACE OF MIND, AND DAILY HAPPINESS

Professional Self-Care

Professional self-care refers to activities that promote a healthy work-life balance, prevent career burnout, and help you to stay satisfied with your working life. Here are some examples of professional self-care activities:

> ➤ Effective time management can help you prioritize your work and prevent you from becoming too stressed out.
>
> ➤ Setting clear boundaries between work and personal life can help you prevent burnout, and assist in improving your overall health.
>
> ➤ Taking regular breaks throughout the workday can help reduce your stress levels, and improve your focus and productivity.
>
> ➤ Seeking opportunities for professional development can help you build your skills and knowledge to improve your job satisfaction.
>
> ➤ Practicing self-reflection can help you decide on and update your career goals and values.
>
> ➤ Seeking support from co-workers, mentors, or a therapist can help you manage work-related stress and navigate career challenges.
>
> ➤ Engaging in activities outside of work (e.g., exercise or hobbies) can help you recharge and reduce burnout.

Environmental Self-Care

Environmental self-care relates to activities that promote a sense of connection and responsibility towards the natural environment. It involves taking steps to reduce our impact on the environment and promote sustainable living. The following are examples of environmental self-care activities:

- ➢ Reducing waste, reusing materials, and recycling.
- ➢ Conserving energy by turning off lights and electronics when we're not using them, using energy-efficient appliances, and using less water can help us reduce our carbon footprint.
- ➢ Spending time in nature—such as hiking or gardening—can promote a sense of connection to the environment and emphasize the need to take care of the earth as our home.
- ➢ Supporting businesses that prioritize sustainability and environmentally friendly practices.
- ➢ Using eco-friendly products (such as reusable bags, water bottles, and cleaning products) can help reduce waste, and also promotes sustainable living.
- ➢ Participating in community clean-up events, such as beach or park clean-ups, can help reduce litter and promote a sense of community responsibility towards the environment.

Managing Disappointment and Sad Situations

Disappointment is a feeling of sadness, frustration, or dissatisfaction that we can feel when our hopes and expectations aren't met. We could feel mild to severe disappointment, depending on the situation. One way to minimize, or prevent, disappointment is to set reasonable goals for ourselves; they should be within our reach, but it should take some effort to achieve them.

Causes of Disappointment

Disappointment can be caused by many different factors. The first seeds for disappointment are usually sown when our expectations aren't met. For instance, we expect to get top marks on an exam, but then we end up failing one of our subjects—or we expect to get a promotion at work, but then it goes to someone else.

We may also feel disappointed when we make plans that don't work out—for example, if we plan an event or a day out that we have to cancel because of unforeseen circumstances.

We may also have had unrealistic expectations that caused disappointment in our lives. For example, if you set over-optimistic expectations for yourself to achieve something in a very short amount of time, you may feel disappointed when you fail to achieve your goals.

If we have a personal attachment to a situation or outcome, we may even face greater disappointment when we fail or if something goes wrong. For example, we could feel a deep sense of disappointment when we're emotionally invested in a relationship and it ends.

Dealing with Disappointment in an Emotionally Intelligent Way

Dealing with disappointment maturely involves being aware of and regulating your emotions, empathizing with others, and adapting to the situation.

One of the first things you need to do is recognize and acknowledge your emotions. Allow yourself to feel disappointed, but try not to dwell on negative emotions.

Recognize that disappointment is a normal part of life, and tell yourself that it's okay to feel upset.

Next, identify what is causing your disappointment. Is it a result of unmet expectations, a change in circumstances, or something else?

Understanding the cause can help you process your emotions and move forward.

Practice empathy and try to understand others' perspectives. This can help you see the bigger picture and may lead to a more positive outcome.

Attempt to reframe your thinking and look for the positives in the situation. For instance, if a project you were working on went wrong, focus on what you learned from the situation and how you can improve in the future.

Think about the steps you can take to move forward and take action. This can help you feel more in control of the situation and may lead to a more positive outcome.

Try to alleviate your disappointment by taking part in activities that make you feel good. This could be anything from exercising to spending time with friends or engaging in a hobby.

SELF-CARE, PEACE OF MIND, AND DAILY HAPPINESS

Dealing with Disappointment—Michael Jordan's Story

Famous basketball player Michael Jordan had to deal with a lot of disappointment in his life. Although Jordan is widely regarded as one of the greatest basketball players of all time, he faced many setbacks and disappointments throughout his career.

One example is the 1994-1995 NBA season when Jordan came out of retirement to play for the Chicago Bulls. Despite his legendary status as a player, Jordan struggled to perform at the same level as he had before his retirement, and the Bulls were eliminated from the playoffs in the second round.

Jordan later described this time as one of the most difficult periods in his life, both on a professional and personal level. He felt the weight of public scrutiny and criticism for his performance, and he also had to face personal challenges such as the murder of his father and a divorce from his wife.

Jordan decided to use his professional disappointment as motivation to come back even stronger. He worked hard to improve his skills and fitness and helped the Bulls to win three more NBA championships.

Jordan's resilience and determination have made him a role model for athletes and non-athletes alike. His story is a reminder that setbacks and failures are a natural part of life, but with hard work and perseverance, it's possible to overcome them and achieve success.

How to Ensure Your Peace of Mind Every Day

Peace of mind is a state of inner calm and tranquility, in which a person is free from worries, anxiety, and stress.

Possessing it enables you to feel content, satisfied, and have mental clarity—which will help you to feel grounded and centered. Having peace of mind will benefit your overall health and well-being as it will help reduce your stress levels, improve your focus and concentration, and make you feel happier and more content.

In these busy, stressful times, it's not easy to find inner peace. However, mindfulness and meditation are powerful tools that can help you find your inner harmony and tranquility.

Mindfulness and Meditation for Inner Peace

Mindfulness helps you to be fully present and engaged in the current moment. You need to pay attention to your thoughts, feelings, and surroundings without judging them. By practicing mindfulness, you can become more aware of your internal experiences, and develop inner calm and clarity.

Meditation is a technique for training the mind and promoting relaxation and inner peace. There are many different types of meditation; most involve focusing your attention on a particular object, such as your breath or a mantra. By focusing your mind in this way, you can quiet your thoughts, and promote a sense of calm and relaxation.

You can combine the two techniques to achieve inner peace. Here are some tips for getting started:

> - Sit in a quiet place, where others won't interrupt you.
> - Your back must be straight and your feet should be flat on the floor.
> - Close your eyes and focus your attention on your breathing; take some deep breaths.

- **Mindfulness** – Bringing your attention to your thoughts, feelings, and bodily sensations. Notice them without judgment, and allow them to come and go.
- **Meditation** – Focus your attention on a particular object, such as your breath. Whenever your mind wanders, gently bring it back to the object of your focus.
- Continue practicing mindfulness and meditation for as long as you feel comfortable.

The key to achieving inner peace through mindfulness and meditation is to practice regularly and be patient with yourself. With time and dedication, you can develop a greater sense of inner calm and tranquility that will enhance your overall well-being.

Daily Exercises for Happiness

Certain things that we do every day can contribute to our overall happiness. Being kind is one of the things that can make us happier in life, and can boost our mood immediately.

Engaging in Acts of Kindness

Performing acts of kindness can give a sense of purpose and meaning to our lives, as we feel that we're contributing positively to the world. It can also enhance our social connections, strengthen our relationships, and help us form new connections.

Being kind to others can also enhance our sense of empathy and compassion, which will enhance our overall well-being, and will also help our relationships with others. Doing something nice for someone else also gives you less time to worry about your own problems, thereby helping to reduce stress levels.

Engaging in Physical Exercise to Boost Your Mood

Not surprisingly, daily physical exercise will also boost your mood. Regular exercise is a powerful tool for improving one's mood, reducing stress, and promoting overall happiness. It works best if you can schedule exercise as a normal part of your daily routine, and you don't have to go out of your way to exercise. For example, walk to work and back, take the stairs rather than the elevator, or dance at social events.

The following exercises can improve your mood and well-being by releasing the brain's feel-good neurotransmitters–endorphins:

- Aerobic exercises like jogging, cycling, or dancing get your heart rate up and release endorphins–the body's natural feel-good chemicals.
- Yoga combines physical activity with mindfulness—helping to reduce stress, increase flexibility and balance, and improve your overall wellness.
- Strength training, like building muscle through weightlifting or bodyweight exercises, can boost your confidence and self-esteem, which are both important for your happiness.
- You can walk anywhere at any time and it can boost your mood and fitness. It can raise your spirits, reduce stress, and increase your energy levels.
- Tai Chi is a gentle, low-impact form of exercise that combines movement and mindfulness and has been shown to reduce stress and improve mood.
- High-Intensity Interval Training (HIIT) workouts consist of short periods of activity, followed by rest periods. This type of

> exercise is an efficient way to improve fitness and can boost mood and energy levels.
> ➤ Dancing is a fun and social activity that can improve your mood and reduce your stress levels.

Consistency is the key to happiness. Make exercise a regular part of your routine, and you'll start to see the benefits over time. Start with just a few minutes a day, and gradually increase the duration and intensity of your workouts. Consult your doctor before you start a new workout routine, especially if you suffer from health conditions.

Engaging in Gratitude

Practicing gratitude is a powerful tool to increase your overall well-being and happiness. The key is to start small and build gradually on your happiness.

Identify one thing that you are grateful for, every day. This doesn't have to be an amazing event or occurrence but can be something simple such as finding a good book you've been wanting to read for a long time, passing a difficult test, or enjoying a piece of cake.

Make it a habit to set aside some time daily to think about what you're grateful for. This could be any time that works for you: before bedtime, early in the morning, or whenever you get the opportunity to take a break.

Keep a journal in which you write down some things you're grateful for, at least weekly. Look back at it, especially if you can't find anything to be grateful for on difficult days.

This can help you focus on the positive aspects of your life, and assist you in building a more positive attitude.

It's important to share your thankfulness with others, and this will also help you forge closer relationships with them.

Express your appreciation in person, or send notes or electronic messages.

Cultivate gratitude through intentional action. By focusing on the positive aspects of your life and expressing appreciation for them, you can increase your overall sense of well-being, and find greater joy and fulfillment in your life.

Brené Brown and Gratitude

Brené Brown is a research professor at the University of Houston and has written several bestselling books on topics such as vulnerability, shame, and courage.

In her book *The Gifts of Imperfection*, Brown writes that most of the people she interviewed who lived joyful lives attributed their happiness to their habit of practicing gratitude.

Brown emphasizes that gratitude is not just a feeling, but a practice that requires intentional effort.

She encourages people to create a daily gratitude practice, such as writing down three things they are grateful for each day, to cultivate a mindset of gratitude and joy.

She has become a well-known advocate for the power of gratitude to transform our lives and increase our sense of well-being.

Key Takeaways

- Taking care of yourself is vital for maintaining good physical, emotional and mental health.
- Self-care isn't selfish, as it's about maintaining good health and preventing burnout.
- Self-care can also help you keep a positive outlook on life.
- Neglecting self-care can lead to negative consequences, such as poor health and decreased productivity.
- Taking care of yourself is not only beneficial for you but also for those around you.
- The different types of self-care include physical, emotional, social, spiritual, intellectual, professional, and environmental self-care.
- Physical self-care is about looking after your body and physical well-being.
- Emotional self-care involves becoming involved in activities that will help you manage your stress, anxiety, and other negative emotions.
- Social self-care is about getting involved with activities that help you form healthy relationships and connections with others.
- Spiritual self-care encompasses exploring and nurturing your spiritual beliefs and practices.
- Intellectual self-care refers to activities that stimulate your mind and challenge you intellectually.

- Professional self-care helps you focus on promoting a healthy work-life balance and preventing career burnout.

- Environmental self-care refers to activities that help you connect to nature and feel a sense of responsibility toward it.

- We can experience disappointment when our expectations aren't met.

- Unrealistic expectations could cause us to become disappointed with life.

- To deal with disappointment in an emotionally intelligent way, you need to be aware of your feelings and be able to regulate them. You need to be able to adapt to situations.

- Meditation can help you relax and find inner peace.

- Engaging in acts of kindness can give your life purpose and meaning. Doing nice things for other people leaves you with less time to worry about your problems.

- Engaging in physical exercise can boost your mood. The best approach is to try a variety of different exercises, and then choose the type that suits you best and stick to it.

- Make exercise a consistent part of your routine, and you'll see the benefits over time.

- Cultivating a sense of gratitude can increase your overall wellness over time. Make it a habit to set aside time to think about what you're grateful for.

Activity: Create a Self-Care Plan

A self-care plan can help you prioritize your needs and make time for activities that promote health and relaxation. Self-care should never be seen as selfish. It's an essential part of maintaining your health and well-being. If you look after yourself well, you'll have more energy to care for the important people in your life, such as your life partner and children.

Follow the steps below to develop a practical self-care plan:

- Start writing your self-care plan by listing the areas of your life that need attention. This can include your physical health, emotional well-being, social connections, spiritual practice, and intellectual growth. We often tend to pay attention to one or two areas, while neglecting the others. However, for the sake of our overall wellness, we need to take care of ourselves in all areas of our lives.

- Take a look at your current routines and habits. Identify areas where you are neglecting self-care, or engaging in habits that are harmful to your well-being. Write down what changes you could implement to improve the situation.

- Set achievable goals for each area of self-care that you want to improve. For example, if you want to prioritize your physical health, you could set a goal to exercise for 30 minutes, three times a week.

- Make time for self-care activities by creating a schedule that includes specific times for each activity. This can help you stay accountable and make self-care a priority. We often make a mental note that we're going to do something, but if we don't schedule it, it's no longer a priority, especially if we're extremely busy and focus our attention on other things that start to seem more important.

➢ Self-care activities can vary widely, so choose the ones that work for you. This can include exercise, meditation, journaling, spending time with loved ones, or taking part in hobbies you enjoy.

➢ Self-care is a process, and it's important to be kind to yourself along the way. If you slip up or struggle to stick to your plan, practice self-compassion and recommit to your goals.

➢ Evaluate your self-care plan from time to time to see what's working and where changes may be needed. It doesn't help you in any way to continue engaging in activities that you have to force yourself to do—for example, a certain type of exercise that you don't enjoy, as you'll just stop doing it in the long term.

CONCLUSION

Developing self-love is a lifelong journey requiring dedication, commitment, and a willingness to be vulnerable and honest with ourselves. Through the pages of this book, you have learned that it's not selfish and indulgent to take care of yourself, but an essential part of living a healthy and fulfilling life. If we love ourselves, we're usually also able to give more of ourselves to others.

If you haven't started your journey of self-appreciation yet, keep in mind that it's never too late to start. Maybe you didn't get your journey to self-esteem and confidence off on the right foot, but it's still possible to catch up.

We hope that you've discovered that self-love begins with acceptance and compassion for yourself. That includes your flaws and imperfections.

Try to let go of the past and embrace the present moment, and cultivate a positive mindset that will empower you to pursue your dreams and live with a newfound purpose.

Liking and loving yourself gives you the power to transform your life from the inside out. You can overcome self-doubt, negative thought patterns, and limiting beliefs—and create a life that is aligned with your deepest desires and values.

Practicing self-love is not a quick fix but needs to be practiced daily, and for the rest of your life. It requires prioritizing your needs and to treating yourself with the same kindness, compassion, and respect that you show to others.

As you continue on your journey, remember to be patient and gentle with yourself. You won't be successful overnight, and it will take work, time, and courage to get to where you want to be. Think of it as a lifelong journey; something that goes hand-in-hand with a lifelong learning mentality.

Celebrate your progress, and forgive yourself for any setbacks or mistakes. Above all, remember that you are worthy of love, happiness, and success; and, it's up to you to create the life you deserve.

We've given you the advice and tools, and now it's up to you to get out there and use them. If you get stuck at any point in your journey, remember to refer back to this guide. It will remind you what you need to do at the different stages of your adventure.

If you have enjoyed this book, we would appreciate it if you could leave a review on Amazon.

ABOUT THE AUTHOR

Dylan Walker is an author and publishing entrepreneur. He lives in California with his wife and three children. He is passionate about health, wellness, simple living, and minimalism.

Dylan has spent many years focusing on healthy relationships, personal growth, and how to manage stress. His aim in writing these books is to help people reach their fullest potential with scientifically proven practices and to empower people from all backgrounds to improve their mental and physical well-being.

His mission is to help as many people as possible by sharing his comprehensive knowledge about living a physically and emotionally healthy lifestyle and forming and maintaining meaningful relationships.

You will enjoy Dylan's practical books if you are committed to improving your life for the long term.

THANK YOU

Thank you so much for purchasing this book.

You could have picked from dozens of other books but you took a chance and chose this one.

So THANK YOU for getting this book and for reading it all the way to the end.

Before you go, I wanted to ask you for one small favor. **Could you please consider posting a review on Amazon? Posting a review is the best and easiest way to support the work of independent authors like me.**

Your feedback will also help me to keep writing the kind of books that will help you get the results you want. It would mean a lot to me to hear from you.

>> **Leave a review on Amazon US** <<

>> **Leave a review on Amazon UK** <<

REFERENCES

Abrams, A. (n.d.). *The arduous journey to self-love.* Vunela. https://www.vunela.com/the-arduous-journey-to-self-love/

Afridi, S. (2021, March 5). *What self-love really is (and isn't).* Live Healthy. https://www.livehealthymag.com/what-self-love-really-is-and-isnt/

Allen, D. (2019, November 20). *Figuring out what success really means to you.* Entrepreneur. https://www.entrepreneur.com/leadership/figuring-out-what-success-really-means-to-you/340819

Ayodeji. (2016, April 26). *The secret to figuring out if your dream is worth following is answering one question.* Ayo, the Writer. https://www.ayothewriter.com/how-to-work-on-your-dream/

Berged, J. (2021, July 19). *How to turn your inner critic into an ally.* Medium. https://medium.com/playground-beyou/how-to-turn-your-inner-critic-into-an-ally-2a51882c28f8

Borenstein, J. (2020, February 12). *Self-love and what it means.* The Brain & Behavior Research Foundation. https://www.bbrfoundation.org/blog/self-love-and-what-it-means

Cherry, K. (2022a, November 14). *What is the negativity bias?* Verywell Mind. https://www.verywellmind.com/negative-bias-4589618

Cherry, K. (2022b, July 22). *5 reasons emotions are important.* Verywell Mind. https://www.verywellmind.com/the-purpose-of-emotions-2795181

Cohn, M. A., Fredrickson, B. L., Brown, S. L., Mikels, J. A., & Conway, A. M. (2009). Happiness unpacked: Positive emotions increase life satisfaction by building resilience. *Emotion, 9*(3), 361–368. https://doi.org/10.1037/a0015952

Constantino, T. (2015, August 27). *5 Dream killers keeping you from the life you could have.* Entrepreneur. https://www.entrepreneur.com/living/5-dream-killers-keeping-you-from-the-life-you-could-have/249959

Davies, E. (2019, July 11). *What is self-neglect?* Ann Craft Trust. https://www.anncrafttrust.org/what-is-self-neglect/

Devries, L. (2022, March 8). *For people who look in the mirror and cringe.* Tiny Buddha. https://tinybuddha.com/blog/for-people-who-look-in-the-mirror-and-cringe/

The Editors of Encyclopaedia Britannica. (2023a, April 4). Michael Jordan. In *Encyclopædia Britannica.* Retrieved April 13, 2023, from https://www.britannica.com/biography/Michael-Jordan

The Editors of Encyclopaedia Britannica. (2023b, April 5). Oprah Winfrey. In *Encyclopædia Britannica.* Retrieved April 13, 2023, from https://www.britannica.com/biography/Oprah-Winfrey

REFERENCES

Eldemire, A. (2019, June 12). Self-love is the new #RelationshipGoals. *Psychology Today.* https://www.psychologytoday.com/us/blog/couples-thrive/201906/self-love-is-the-new-relationshipgoals?amp

Eliassen, R. (2021, March 11). *Undo these 14 cognitive distortions to reduce your negative thoughts.* Medium. https://medium.com/mind-cafe/undo-these-14-cognitive-distortions-to-reduce-your-negative-thoughts-b2bc54bc3383

Eminem Biography. (n.d.). Eminem.net. https://www.eminem.net/biography/

Emma Stone. (2022, October 11). National Today. https://nationaltoday.com/birthday/emma-stone/

Fabrega, M. (2017, April 2). *Ten ways to declutter your mind and free up mental space.* Daring to Live Fully. https://daringtolivefully.com/declutter-your-mind

Felman, A. (2020, July 20). *25 science-backed ways to take better care of yourself.* Greatist. https://greatist.com/happiness/ways-to-practice-self-care

Frothingham, S. (2019, December 16). *What is negativity bias, and how does it affect you?* Healthline. https://www.healthline.com/health/negativity-bias

Gavin, M. L. (2021, January 29). *The power of positive emotions.* KidsHealth. https://kidshealth.org/en/teens/power-positive.html

Golden, B. (2022, April 30). *Overcoming toxic emotions.* Shoreline Media Group. https://www.shorelinemedia.net/white_lake_beacon/lifestyle/faith/overcoming-toxic-emotions/article_91316a6e-f133-55c6-850f-a4a18a60839f.html

Hooks, E. J. (2017, February 28). *What self-love is not and why it matters.* Emily J. Hooks. https://emilyjhooks.com/self-love-matters/

Hunt, G. (2019, August 6). *Self love... oh cringe!* Gemma Hunt Therapy. https://www.gemmahunttherapy.com/post/self-love-oh-cringe

Hurley, K. (2022, July 14). *What is resilience? Your guide to facing life's challenges, adversities, and crises.* Everyday Health. https://www.everydayhealth.com/wellness/resilience/

James McAvoy. (2022, November 21) National Today. https://nationaltoday.com/birthday/james-mcavoy/

Keeping it awkward, brave, and kind. (2023, March 1). Brené Brown. https://brenebrown.com/

Khan, Z. Z. (2023, April 6). *The importance of self-love.* The Daily Star. https://www.thedailystar.net/lifestyle/reader%E2%80%99s-chit/news/the-importance-self-love-1684162?amp

Kolonko, C. (2022, April 14). *How does self-esteem relate to depression?* Psych Central. https://psychcentral.com/depression/is-low-self-esteem-making-you-vulnerable-to-depression

Lancer, D. (2011, August 2). *How do self-love, self-esteem, self-acceptance differ?* What Is Codependency. https://whatiscodependency.com/self-acceptance-vs-self-love-vs-self-esteem/

Lauren, J. (2016, July 20). *What success really means.* HuffPost. https://www.huffpost.com/entry/what-success-really-means_b_11077434/amp

REFERENCES

Martin, M. (2021, April 1). *Self-Care isn't selfish*. This Is It Network. https://thisisittv.com/self-care-isnt-selfish/

Maté, G. (2022, April 1). *In the realm of hungry ghosts*. Dr. Gabor Maté. https://drgabormate.com/book/in-the-realm-of-hungry-ghosts/

McCarthy, M. (2019, August 8). *Why strong self-esteem is the secret to success in life*. Createwritenow. https://www.createwritenow.com/journal-writing-blog/why-strong-self-esteem-is-the-secret-to-success-in-life

Miller, K. (2023, February 17). *Selena Gomez just explained how Lupus medication affects her body*. SELF. https://www.self.com/story/selena-gomez-lupus-medication-side-effects

Moulder, H. (2022, July 6). *How to be successful and happy at the same time*. Course Correction Coaching. https://www.coursecorrectioncoaching.com/how-to-be-successful-happy/

Nazish, N. (2017, November 19). How to declutter your mind: 10 practical tips you'll actually want to try. *Forbes*. https://www.forbes.com/sites/nomanazish/2017/11/19/how-to-declutter-your-mind-10-practical-tips-youll-actually-want-to-try/amp/

Patel, D. (2017, February 23). *18 Destructive habits holding you back from success*. Entrepreneur. https://www.entrepreneur.com/leadership/18-destructive-habits-holding-you-back-from-success/288411

Ruiz, M. (2021, February 13). I love myself. Why is that so hard to say out loud? *Vogue.* https://www.vogue.com/article/i-love-myself-why-is-that-so-hard-to-say-out-loud

Sandoiu, A. (2018, March 23). *Why self-love is important and how to cultivate it.* Medical News Today. https://www.medicalnewstoday.com/articles/321309

Scott, C. (2022, May 3). *Self-love is vital for any type of success.* Addicted2Success. https://addicted2success.com/success-advice/self-love-is-vital-for-any-type-of-success/

Soken-Huberty, E. (2021, April 17). *10 reasons why self-love is important.* The Important Site. https://theimportantsite.com/10-reasons-why-self-love-is-important/

Stanborough, R. J. (2022, October 25). *What are cognitive distortions and how can you change these thinking patterns?* Healthline. https://www.healthline.com/health/cognitive-distortions

Tikkanen, A. (2023, April 4). Lizzo. In *Encyclopedia Britannica.* Retrieved April 13, 2023, from https://www.britannica.com/biography/Lizzo

Toomey, A. (2014, October 29). *Jennifer Lopez admits she's felt "abused" in past relationships, reveals the moment she decided to divorce Marc Anthony.* E! News. https://www.eonline.com/news/593024/jennifer-lopez-admits-she-s-felt-abused-in-past-relationships-reveals-the-moment-she-decided-to-divorce-marc-anthony

Touronis, V. (2021, August 27). *How to stop negative thoughts that cause anxiety.* My Online Therapy. https://myonlinetherapy.com/how-to-stop-negative-thoughts-anxiety/

REFERENCES

WebMD Editorial Contributors Brennan, D. (2021, October 25) *Mental health benefits of decluttering.* WebMD. https://www.webmd.com/mental-health/mental-health-benefits-of-decluttering

What causes low self-esteem? Advekit. (n.d.). *Advekit.* https://www.advekit.com/blogs/what-causes-low-self-esteem

The White House. (2016, February 11). *First Lady Michelle Obama.* Whitehouse. https://obamawhitehouse.archives.gov/administration/first-lady-michelle-obama

Williams, K. (2022, April 23). *Self-love isn't selfish: 9 Reasons to start believing.* KB in Bloom. https://kbinbloom.com/self-love-isnt-selfish/

Yost, M. (2021, March 2). *19 definitions of success you should never ignore.* Lifehack. https://www.lifehack.org/articles/communication/the-new-definitions-success.html

Printed in Great Britain
by Amazon

923437d9-7a03-4622-9c21-67626852f821R01